CYPRIOTE SHIPS
from
THE BRONZE AGE TO C. 500 BC

by
Karin Westerberg

Paul Åströms förlag
Gothenburg 1983

ABSTRACT

The study deals with clay models, graffiti on stones and vase paintings of ships of Cypriote manufacture from the Bronze Age to c. 500 BC. The material is catalogued and described. This is the essence of the study. Even if most items in the catalogue are grave finds, the study does not deal with funeral customs and traditions but exclusively with the vessel from navigation and construction points of view.

The graffiti on stones are only roughly outlined, and with few exceptions the clay models are crudely made, with very few details.

An attempt to classify the ships according to certain characteristics such as size, hull, rigging and function is included, as well as a description of the way in which they were built. The primitiveness of the material has prevented too far-reaching conclusions being drawn. Certain comparisons, however, have been made with what is known from other parts of the eastern Mediterranean and with the ships from the Homeric poetry. These comparisons indicate that we cannot rule out the possibility that the Cypriote ships also were built by the shell method, i.e. the hull was first raised and then the reinforcement inserted. Furthermore most of the ships in the catalogue, and presumably most ships, were in reality propelled by a combination of sails and oars. The ships in this study have mainly been interpreted as representations of ships made and used for peaceful purposes. The size and the qualities of some of the ships are telling arguments for their ability to cross the seas and can be seen as evidence of the central role of Cyprus in international trade.

Westerberg, K., *Cypriote Ships from The Bronze Age to c. 500 BC: Studies in Mediterranean Archaeology,* Pocket-book 22, Gothenburg 1983. Published by Paul Åström, Gothenburg, Sweden. Thesis from the Department of Ancient Culture and Civilization, Gothenburg University.

Key words: Archaeology, Cyprus, Bronze Age, Cypro-Geometric, Cypro-Archaic, ship-models.

CONTENTS

PREFACE

The preparation of this study has, during the last years, been both interesting and varied and to a great degree has brought a new stimulus into my life. Without the constant help of my husband, my true companion, it would not have been possible to complete it. I have been given the opportunity not only to study the ship models of the great museums, the British Museum, the Musée du Louvre and the Cyprus Museum of Nicosia, but also to search for models in the smaller local museums in Cyprus and – for example – to visit a Limassol ship-broker, owner of one of the most advanced models. It is impossible to describe my feelings when, by pure chance, I happened to find a Cypriote ship model at the Archaeological Museum of Istanbul! Unforgettable cruises in large and small sailing yachts with my husband in the Aegean archipelago have given me a practical experience of Mediterranean conditions.

I am highly indebted to Mr. Vassos Karageorghis and the staff at the Cyprus Museum, to Mr. D.M. Bailey at the British Museum and to the staff at the Musée du Louvre and at the Metropolitan Museum of Art for their kind help and for giving me access to their store-rooms.

The study has benefited from scrutiny and discussion by members of the Seminar of the Department of Ancient Culture and Civilization of the University of Gothenburg.

I am grateful to Verlag Philipp von Zabern, Mainz am Rhein, for giving me permission to publish photographs Nos. 158 and 166 from the book by A. Göttlicher and to Mrs. Marie Stenberg for all her help in typing the manuscript.

I am also very much indebted to Mr. George R. Otter, who has kindly checked my English in this study.

Finally I want to thank my tutor Professor Paul Åström for suggesting a thesis so much in keeping with one of my main spheres of interest. His encouraging suggestions and kind support have always been an invaluable asset in my work.

Gothenburg
December 1982

Karin Westerberg

ABBREVIATIONS

AA	*Archäologischer Anzeiger*, Berlin.
AJA	*American Journal of Archaeology*, New York.
Altägäis und Altkypros	H.–G. Buchholz and V. Karageorghis, *Altägäis und Altkypros*, Tübingen 1971.
BCH	*Bulletin de Correspondance Hellénique*, Paris.
BMC	H.B. Walters, *Catalogue of the Greek and Etruscan vases in the British Museum*, London 1912.
Casson	L. Casson, *Ships and seamanship in the ancient world*, Princeton, NJ, 1971.
CT	H. B. Walters, *Catalogue of the terracottas in the Department of Greek and Roman Antiquities, British Museum*, London 1903.
CVA	*Corpus Vasorum Antiquorum*.
Dikaios	P. Dikaios, *A guide to the Cyprus Museum*, 3, rev. ed. Nicosia 1961.
Gray	D. Gray, *Seewesen*, Göttingen 1974 (=*Archaeologia Homerica*, Band I, Kap. G.)
Göttlicher	A. Göttlicher, *Materialen für ein Corpus der Schiffsmodelle im Altertum*, Mainz 1977.
HST	*Hala Sultan Tekke*, Gothenburg, *SIMA* XLV.
JFA	*Journal of Field Archaeology*, Boston.
JHS	*The Journal of Hellenic Studies*, London.
LC	Late Cypriote Bronze Age.
L.o.a.	length over all.
Merrillees	R.S. Merrillees, *The Cypriote Bronze Age pottery found in Egypt*, Lund 1968, (*SIMA* XVIII).
Murray	A.S. Murray, A. H. Smith, H. B. Walters, *Excavations in Cyprus*. First published 1900, Photolithographic reprint, London 1970.
RDAC	*Report of the Department of Antiquities, Cyprus*, Nicosia.
SCE	*The Swedish Cyprus Expedition*, Stockholm, Lund.
SIMA	*Studies in Mediterranean Archaeology*, Lund, Gothenburg.

INTRODUCTION

Since time immemorial the sea and the rivers have been increasingly important for inter-state communications. Across the sea, culture has spread and innovations have been borne. Until the past century travelling by sea was the natural way of communicating between most countries in the Mediterranean area. Through archaeological finds and written evidence, the peoples around the Nile, the Euphrates and the Tigris stand out as the inventors of the ship, succeeded by Cretans, Mycenaeans, Phoenicians and Greeks. Undoubtedly other peoples along the shores of the Mediterranean as well as the inhabitants of the islands have contributed just as much. Knowledge of ship-building was not exclusive but widely understood.

Cyprus is the third in size of the islands of the Mediterranean and situated at the intersection of the cultural and commercial spheres of three continents. Its geographical position is a condition for trade and shipping which were as active as those of Crete and the Aegean islands. For several decades intensive research has been conducted into the history of Cyprus. In this connection, trade and shipping have been discussed[1], as well as the prerequisites for ship-building – availability of suitable material and technical skill. The spread of Cypriote pottery in the eastern Mediterranean area has been surveyed, as well as the occurrence of foreign pottery on Cyprus.

Trade with perishable products such as wood, wine, oil etc., can be difficult to prove. On the other hand, obsidian findings have given proof that communications by sea took place as early as before 6000 BC. Obsidian has been found at nearly every Neolithic site in the eastern Mediterranean, although in very small quantities at sites far from Melos and the Anatolian sources. On Cyprus, so far, obsidian blades have been found at Khirokitia, Troulli, Petra tou Limniti, Cape Andreas, Kalavassos-Tenta and Lemba Lakkous.[2] Even if there is no more direct evidence preserved this shipping may have been undertaken by primitive dugouts, probably by a process of "island-hopping". Marine contacts seem to have been very rare during the Neolithic period and the Early Bronze Age, as the art of ship-building was still at a very low stage. The decisive technical steps in ship-building were not taken until the second millennium BC, when mast and sails became more generally used.[3]

4

Further evidence of the position of Cyprus as a commercial and shipping centre during the late Bronze Age is given by D. McCaslin's investigation of the numerous stone anchor finds from coastal settlements and from the sea in the eastern Mediterranean.[4] There is nothing to contradict the possibility that the same trading routes were also used during the Iron Age.

The aim of this thesis is to catalogue and discuss the archaeological material consisting of clay models of ships, graffiti and paintings of ships of Cypriote origin from the Bronze and Iron Ages. As so often within this special field the material available has, regrettably, been limited. So far, no finds from Neolithicum and the Early Bronze Age, except possibly No. 4, have, as far as I know, been reported, no doubt for reasons indicated above. This short introduction will be followed by chronology, catalogue with descriptions and glossary of nautical terms. As a conclusion there will then follow a systematization of the material concerning on the one hand certain technical details of the ships such as size, hull, mast, sails etc., and on the other hand characteristics of the ships such as eyes (apotropaic) and other decorations, as well as the size of the crew, followed by an attempt to establish the type of the ship in question, including its seaworthiness and its capability to leave the shore and sail across the seas. I shall also discuss the fundamental but somewhat controversial question of what are stern and bow. As the main part of the material can be dated to Geometric and Archaic times, a comparison must also be made with other finds and with the ships of the Homeric poems. Even if most items in the catalogue are grave finds, my thesis will not deal with funeral customs and traditions but exclusively with the vessel from a navigation and a construction point of view. In this introduction, I also want to mention that I have had the opportunity to measure and to study all the items except those in Poland, U.S.A. and Austria. It also has to be emphasized that when I use the words ships, boats and vessels, this does not imply any estimation regarding size or type but is only for stylistic reasons.

From the period discussed in this study there have unfortunately only been found clay models and graffiti of ships but as yet no real ships. It is possible that future underwater archaeology may discover wrecks which can bring us further knowledge and information.

The fact that the majority of the ships in this cataogue are clay models inevitably brings to mind the story about Kinyras.[5] Kinyras, said to have ruled over Paphos, had, according to Homer, promised Agamemnon to send him 50 ships as reinforcement in the war against Troy. He kept his promise by sending one real ship which brought 49 clay models of ships. Consequently, after the fall of Troy, Agamemnon sailed to Cyprus and banished Kinyras from Paphos to Amathus. – Unlike Agamemnon, I should have been very grateful for one single real ship from this period as a source of information!

NOTES: INTRODUCTION

1. E. Gjerstad, *SCE* IV:2. 459–460; Merrillees, 187–189; R.S. Merrillees, *Trade and transcendence in the Bronze Age Levant,* Gothenburg 1974, (*SIMA* XXXIX), 5–8; D.E. McCaslin, 'The 1977 underwater report' in *HST* 4, Gothenburg 1978, (*SIMA* XLV:4), 97–137; D.E. McCaslin, *Stone anchors in Antiquity: Coastal settlements and maritime trade – routes in the Eastern Mediterranean ca. 1600–1050 B.C.,* Gothenburg 1980, (*SIMA* LXI), 87–107 for further details.
2. P. Dikaios, *Khirokitia,* London 1953, 316–317; P. Åström, 'Cypern – en kulturhistorisk och konsthistorisk skiss' in *Cypern – motsättningarnas ö,* Gothenburg 1974, (*SIMA* Pocket-book 1), 7; I.A. Todd, 'Vasilikos Valley project: Second preliminary report, 1977,' *JFA* 5, 1978, 179; I.A. Todd, 'Vasilikos Valley project: Third preliminary report 1978', *JFA* 6, 1979, 277, 288; E. J. Peltenburg, *Recent developments in the Later Prehistory of Cyprus,* Gothenburg 1982, (*SIMA* Pocket-book 16), 81.
3. Casson, 38–39.
4. E. McCaslin, (supra note 1), 87–107.
5. Homer, *Iliad,* 11.20.

I CHRONOLOGY

For the Middle and Late Bronze Age or Middle and Late Cypriote I have followed the chronology proposed by Paul Åström in *SCE* IV:1B, 273, and IV:1D, 762. For the Cypro-Geometric and Cypro-Archaic periods I prefer to follow the dates proposed by Gjerstad in *SCE* IV:2, 427 rather than Judy Birmingham's high chronology dating in *AJA* 67, 1963, 15–42.

II CATALOGUE

The catalogue deals exclusively with ships of Cypriote manufacture and with objects and drawings of what without doubt must be considered as ships or parts of ships.

Consequently I have excluded certain items which, by tradition or convention, have sometimes been classified as ships. In the following catalogue I have thus not included imported items, such as a Mycenaean sherd of a clay model of a ship from Amathus, Tomb 17[1], nor a decked merchantman painted on a Mycenaean jar found at Enkomi, Tomb 3.[2]

I have also excluded three vases, sometimes considered to be boat-shaped.[3] I consider the shapes of these vases to be more horn-like and insufficient for classification as ships.

The same doubt applies to a pyxis of White Painted Ware illustrated and mentioned in *Missions en Chypre* by C.F.A. Schaeffer as "Vase en forme de barque?".[4] In this case, Schaeffer also seems to have been somewhat hesitant.

Another controversial group of items are two pairs of firedogs from Salamis and Kouklia. Even if there is a certain maritime touch about them, I have considered such an interpretation too far-fetched to classify them as ships.[5]

Nor have I seen any reasons to include a gem with an unusual Athena who, according to John Boardman, "is holding an aphlaston, the stern of a ship, indicating her concern with the welfare at sea of her clients or recording a victory". [6] It seems to me that the object she is holding is more flower-shaped and has no maritime connection. Furthermore, I have not included graffiti on two limestone ashlar blocks from Hala Sultan Tekke[7] as I have considered the lines inadequate for interpretation as ships.

NOTES: II CATALOGUE

1. The British Museum, London, Inv. No. 9812-I 146; *BMC* C 694; *CVA* BM: 1, Pl. 11, 4; *SCE* IV:1 C, 382; *SCE* IV:1D, 512.
2. *SCE* I, 484, No. 262.
3. *Altägäis und Altkypros*, 161–162, Nos. 1720–1721; M. Ohnefalsch-Richter, *Kypros, die Bibel und Homer*, Berlin 1893, Pl. IIC, 9 and Pl. CXLV, 3.
4. C.F.Α. Schaeffer, *Missions en Chypre*, Paris 1952, Pl. XXII:2.
5. V. Karageorghis, *Salamis in Cyprus*, London 1969, 91, Plates 51, 52; Gray, G. 24, 13.
6. J. Boardman, *Greek gems and finger rings*, London 1970, 198, Pl. 486.
7. U. Öbrink, *HST* 5, Gothenburg 1979, (*SIMA* XLV:5), 16–17, N 407, Fig. 103 and N 4014, Fig. 104.

A. MIDDLE CYPRIOTE PERIOD

1. Clay model of ship
Fig. 1.
Musée du Louvre, Paris, Inv. No. AM 972.
Provenance: Further provenance in Cyprus unknown.
Regarding the provenance Göttlicher must have been mistaken.
H. Th. Bossert, *Altsyrien,* Tübingen 1951, 8 and No. 111, 39; P. Åström, *The Middle Cypriote Bronze Age,* Lund 1957, 155, 254 and 275 with further references; *Altägäis und Altkypros,* 161, No. 1718; P. Åström, 'Cypern – en kulturhistorisk och konsthistorisk skiss' in *Cypern – motsättningarnas ö,* Gothenburg 1974, (*SIMA* Pocket-book 1), 7, Fig. 6:7; Gray, G. 29, 2.a); Göttlicher, 34, No. 143, Pl. 8; A. Caubet, V. Karageorghis and M. Yon, *Les antiquités de Chypre, Age du Bronze,* Paris 1981, (Musée du Louvre, Département des antiquités orientales, Notes et Documents des musées de France 2), 25 and 81.
L.o.a. 25 cm.
Beam amidships between gunwales 7 cm.
Beam amidships at waterline 11 cm.
Height amidships 8 cm.
The ship is made in White Painted II Ware.
The design of the decoration is geometrical in dark colour. The surface of the hull is smooth. The bottom of the hull is rounded. The two stems project 4 and 3 cm respectively from the gunwale. On each side of the hull, approximately amidships, the gunwale has been pierced. The two holes, one 0.5 cm and the other 0.2 cm, are not placed exactly opposite each other. There are eight human figures sitting on the gunwale, including one figure riding on the stem. The figures are about 8 cm high and made in the "snow-man" technique, i.e. with topped caps and protruding noses, chins and ears. There are no indications of their sex. The figures are evenly placed around the gunwale, except one pair sitting close together with their arms around each other. One figure is resting his arm on the stem and another makes a gesture with one of his arms towards the top of his head. Eyes, nostrils and mouths are marked by holes. Between the human figures there is, on each side of the hull, a small birdlike object about 1.5 cm high perched on the gunwale. All around the hull the upper part of the gunwale is curved slightly inwards, creating fore and aft a kind of small deck or shelter. The ship has no interior fittings. The decoration of the hull is made in two areas divided by two horizontal, parallel lines along the waterline. The area below

9

these lines is decorated with a cross-hatched pattern and the upper area between the horizontal lines and the gunwale, with a zigzag pattern. This area is limited upwards by another horizontal line following the gunwale. Also the human figures and the "birds" are decorated with horizontal stripes. On some of the figures the painted cap-stripes have been replaced by clay stripes.

The model is of Middle Cypriote I date.

2. Sherds of clay model of ship.

Fig. 2.

Cyprus Museum, Nicosia, Inv. No. 1941/III – 6/1 and 1941/1 – 18/1.

Provenance: The sherds were purchased by the Department of Antiquities of Cyprus and were found in a tomb at Politiko, *Lambertis*.

D. Frankel, 'A Middle Cypriote vessel with modelled figures from Politiko, *Lambertis*', *RDAC* 1974, 43–50.

The sherds are of White Painted IV Ware.

As these sherds represent only a small part of the original ship, it is difficult to draw any conclusions regarding the shape of the hull. The material also includes four small White Painted Ware anthropomorphic figures. I agree, however, with David Frankel that this ship may have been similar to the above mentioned one at the Louvre Museum.

The sherds are of Middle Cypriote Bronze Age II or III date.

3. Clay model of ship.

Fig. 3.

British Museum, London, Inv. No. C 261.

Provenance: Further provenance in Cyprus unknown.

CT I, 2, 49, Fig. 84; Gray, G. 19, 45; Göttlicher, 34, No. 148.

L.o.a. 12,7 cm

The model is of White Painted IV Ware.

The bottom of the hull is rounded. On each side of the hull the gunwale has been pierced in groups of two holes, except in the bow where there is one hole on each side.

The function of these holes is not clear. They could either be a suspension device or an arrangement for fastening the cargo. There is a human figure seated in the stern, leaning backwards. Compared with other items this figure is surprisingly lifelike. The item has much in common with Nos. 1 and 2 supra.

The model is of Middle Cypriote III date.

4. Clay model of ship.
Fig. 4.
Musée du Louvre, Paris, Inv. No. AO 17521.
Provenance: Further provenance in Cyprus unknown.
A. Caubet, V. Karageorghis and M. Yon, *Les antiquités de Chypre, Age du Bronze,* Paris 1981, (Musée du Louvre, Département des antiquités orientales, Notes et Documents des musées de France 2), 10 and 74, suggesting Vounous as possible site of origin.
L.o.a. 33 cm.
Beam amidships 21 cm.
Height amidships to the gunwale 16 cm.

The model is badly damaged, and although only about one fifth of the original material remains an entire ship has been reconstructed. It is of Red Polished Ware III and has incised decoration. The two stems project 2 cm above the gunwale. They have square tops and are pierced with a hole. The deck is convex with a rectangular hole, 8.5 x 7 cm, in the middle. Only a small part of the hole is original.

I doubt if any conclusions regarding contemporary hull shapes can be drawn from this item.

The model may be dated to Middle Cypriote or perhaps to Early Cypriote Bronze Age.

B. LATE CYPRIOTE PERIOD

5. Clay model of ship.
Fig. 5.
Cyprus Museum, Nicosia, Inv. No. T 2 B No. 377.
Provenance: Kazaphani Tomb 2 B, No. 377.
BCH 88 (1964) 337, Fig. 70 a, b; *JHS* 85 (1965) Arch. Rep. 1965/66, 29 ff., Fig. 3 a, b; Merrillees, 188; Gray, G. 19, 46 and G. 46, Pl. G. II c, d; Göttlicher, 37, No. 167, Pl. 12.
L.o.a. 45 cm.
Beam amidships 20.5 cm.
Height amidships 15 cm.

The colour of the clay is red and there is no painted decoration. The hull of the model is thin and elegant. It is a big model, almost complete and in very good condition. The hull is canoe-shaped, deep and hollow. The bottom is rounded, with stem markings fore and aft. The stems project, one about 6 cm and the other 2 cm above the gunwale. On the lower one the upper part is missing. It is difficult to decide what is bow and what is stern. A marked protruding stripe runs between the stems and follows the sheer of the hull on both sides. About 1 cm below the gunwale, there is a horizontal line of holes through the planking, running equally spaced from stem to stem, 37 holes on one side and 38 on the other. These holes have been made before firing. Inside the ship between the stems there is a narrow keel-plank, widening towards the stems to a width of about 2 cm. On one of the stems inside the hull there are seven round protruding buttons, 1 cm in diameter. The upper two buttons are at the same level and the other five placed in a vertical row below. It may be presumed that these buttons represent bolts. Exactly amidships there is a clearly marked mast-socket, 3.5 cm high and 3 cm in diameter. On each side of the mast-socket, one 7 cm and the other 9 cm from the keel plank, there is a bollard or belaying pin. One of them is partly damaged.

Parallels to this large clay model are the ones from Maroni, Nos. 6 and 7 infra, although these have not as many interesting details as this one.

The model is dated between the end of LC I and the end of LC II according to the excavator, Dr. Kyriakos Nicolaou. Karageorghis, Gray and Merrillees agree with the dating. Göttlicher may not have observed this, as he dates the model to 600 BC.

6. Clay model of ship.
Fig. 6.
British Museum, London, Inv. No. 98.12–1105.
Provenance: Maroni, *Zarukas,* Site A Tomb 1.
CT, 6, A 49; M. Ohnefalsch-Richter, *Kypros, die Bibel und Homer,* Pl. 168 I c; *JHS* 31 (1911), 112; Merrillees, 188, Pl. XXXVII–2. left; *SCE* IV; 1D, 516 and 585; Gray, G. 20, 47., Pl. G. II a.; Göttlicher, 34, No. 146, Pl. 9; J. Johnson, *Maroni de Chypre,* Gothenburg 1980, (*SIMA* LIX), 15, No. 15, Pl. IX.
L.o.a. 32 cm.
Beam amidships 15 cm.
Height amidships 10 cm.
It is made in Plain White Hand-made Ware and has faint traces of painted decoration. The hull is canoe-shaped, broad and low amidships. The bottom is flattened. Both the stems are damaged and the tops are missing. 1 cm below the gunwale, from stem to stem on each side of the ship there is a horizontal line of 18 pierced holes of equal size. They have been made before firing. About 3 cm below the gunwale, 10 cm from the

stems fore and aft on each side of the ship, there is a roughly cut hole, 1 cm in diameter. Similar holes appear on some other items, for example the clay models Nos. 8 and 32 infra, where they probably served as holes for painters or anchor-lines. In this case, on the other hand, there is nothing to indicate that they have served such a purpose. It seems more probable that they have been used for hanging the ship as suggested in *SCE* IV: 1D, 585, note 7. In the centre amidships there is a mast-socket, 2 x 1.5 cm with an oval depression in the top.

According to the excavator's notes and tomb-lists the ship was full of knuckle-bones when found.

The model is known to be of LC I or II date according to Merrillees. According to *SCE* IV:1D, 516 and 585, the boats from Maroni cannot be safely dated by context. As several features, however, of this ship are similar to those of the Kazaphani ship, No. 5, I feel inclined to date this item to LC I or II. Furthermore, according to Jane Johnson, most material found in Tombs 1 and 7 at Maroni date from LC I and II.

7. *Clay model of ship.*
Fig. 7.
British Museum, London, Inv. No. 98.12–1121.
Provenance: Maroni, *Zarukas,* Site A Tomb 7.
CT, 6, A 50; Merrillees, 188, Pl. XXXVII-2. right; *SCE* IV: 1D, 516 and 585; Gray, G. 20, 48., Pl. G. IIb; Göttlicher, 34, No. 147, Pl. 9; J. Johnson, *Maroni de Chypre,* Gothenburg 1980, (*SIMA* LIX) 18–19, No. 60, Pl. XVI.
L.o.a. 58.7 cm.
Beam amidships 21.5 cm.
Height amidships 14 cm.

It is made in Plain White Hand-made Ware. Outside the hull there are faint traces of white colour. The hull is canoe-shaped, lowest amidships and rising towards the stems. The stems project about 5 cm above the gunwale. The rounded bottom of the hull is repaired and part of it missing. 1 cm immediately below the gunwale on each side of the hull, there is a horizontal line of 18 pierced holes following the sheer. The pierced holes have been made before firing and are of equal size. One of the stems, following the same contour as the keel, ends in an unusual rowlock-like shape. Inside the hull, about 3.5 cm below the gunwale, close to the stem, there is a transverse beam or thwart, 6 cm long and 1.5 cm wide. Roughly amidships, 4.5 cm below the gunwale on each side, there is a console, 2 cm wide and projecting 1.5 cm from the hull. This console is pierced by a vertical hole in the middle and may have served as support for a mast thwart.

The model can be dated in the same way as the above-mentioned No. 6, i.e. to LC I or II.

8. Clay model of ship.
Fig. 8.
Private Collection of Nicos Kirzis, Limassol.
Provenance: Amathus. Found in the sea outside Amathus by fishermen.
It is, as far as I know, not yet published.
L.o.a. 45 cm.
Beam amidships (at water-line) 22 cm.
Beam amidships (between gunwales) 19 cm.
Height from bottom to top of gunwale 15 cm.

The colour of the clay is difficult to tell, as the hull has not yet been washed and is covered by seashells and traces of seaweed. On the port side, however, very faint traces of a black decoration are visible. The ship is in fairly good condition, even if part of the port gunwale and a small part of the bow stem are missing. The hull is rounded and rather clumsy. The ship is massive and most impressive and there are many interesting features. Along the hull immediately below the gunwale there is a row of holes, seven on the port side and eight on the starboard. Some of the holes are square and some more rounded, although the last form could have been shaped by seashells. The bow stem protrudes 3 cm above the gunwale. The stern, which is unusual and most interesting, is formed like some kind of deck-house with a poop-deck and protrudes 6 cm above the gunwale. The deck-house rests on a cross-beam, 9 cm long and 2 cm wide, placed on the gunwale and slightly protruding outside the hull. It is surmounted by a similar cross-beam. Between these two beams there is one pillar on each side, 3 cm high and 2 cm wide. The space between these two pillars creates an entrance to the deck-house. Aft of the pillars there are two triangular windows. Immediately aft of the bow stem there is a cross-beam, 9 cm long and 2 cm wide, placed on the gunwale and slightly protruding outside the hull. An interesting and unusual feature are the four catheads, 1 cm in diameter and protruding 1 cm outside the hull. Two are placed below the bow cross-beam and two below the stern deck-house. Usually, catheads are timbers projecting from the bow to which the anchors are secured. In this case there are two similar timbers projecting from the stern, whose function is not quite clear. They may have had a similar function to the bow ones in securing stern anchors. Their function may also have been to serve as support for the steering oars. The last hypothesis, however, is contradicted by the fact that the stern cross-beam resting on the railing and slightly protruding has distinct hollows on both sides indicating supports for the steering oars. In the middle of the ship there is a mast-socket, 3 cm high and 1.5 cm in diameter. Consequently, it must have been a sailing ship and the row of holes along the hull may have served either as scuppers or as oar-holes.

The model is dated to 1600–1050 BC. It is not safely dated by context. Many features of this ship are similar to those found on the ships from Kazaphani and Maroni, which makes a LC date probable.

9. Clay model of ship.
Fig. 9.
Musées Royaux d'Art et d'Histoire, Brussels, Inv. No. A 1240.
Provenance: Although uncertain, the provenance is supposed to be Enkomi.
Journal of the Royal Anthropological Institute 30, 1900, 199–220; Merrillees, 188, Pl. XXXVII–1; Gray, G. 20, 61; Göttlicher 35, No. 150, Pl. 9.
L.o.a. 18 cm.
Beam amidships 6 cm.
Height amidships 4 cm.
Height from gunwale to top of stem 5.5 cm.

The colour of the clay is grey and there is no painted decoration. The canoe-shaped hull is damaged. The stems are surmounted by identical flat-topped projections. There are no interior fittings.

According to Merrillees and Gray, this item is probably of LC I or II date, even if there are some features similar to those of the ships of Cypro-Archaic date. Göttlicher says 1000 BC. I prefer Merrillees' and Gray's dating.

10. Clay model of ship.
Fig. 10.
Musée du Louvre, Paris, Inv. No. Am 636.
Provenance: Further provenance in Cyprus unknown.
CVA, Louvre 4, II C a, Pl. 2 No. 15; Göttlicher 34, No. 145.
L.o.a. 19 cm.
Beam 8 cm.
Height 8.3 cm.

The colour of the clay is light yellow. The hull is crescent-shaped and there are no interior fittings. Both stems rise above the gunwale, one with a slight resemblance to a bird's head, the other consequently to a bird's tail or perhaps a fish-tail. The item is probably of LC I or II date. It is similar to No. 9 supra.

11. Clay model of ship.

Fig. 11.

Private Collection of Mr. Phr. Nicolaïdès, Limassol.

Provenance: The provenance is uncertain, but it was found in the sea, probably near Amathus.

BCH 100, 1976, 872, Fig. 64.

L.o.a. 26 cm.

Height amidships 2.5 cm.

The colour of the clay is reddish and there is no painted decoration. The hull is slender. Below the gunwale on each side there is a row of twelve round holes of equal size.

The ship has four thwarts of the following sizes:

1. Length 4 cm.   width 1.4 cm.
2. Length 6.4 cm.   width 1.6 cm.
3. Length 5.9 cm.   width 1.6 cm.
4. Length 4.5 cm.   width 1.5 cm.

One of the stems is raised above the gunwale, and is attached to what seems to be a small poop-deck.

The model is said to be of LC date, but it is not safely dated by context. Some features are similar to those above mentioned, but there are also details reminding of items from the Cypro-Archaic period.

12. Amphora with a painted ship.

Fig. 12.

Hadjiprodromou Collection, Famagusta.

Provenance: Between Karavas and Lapithos, the site *Vathyrkakas*.

V. Karageorghis and J. des Gagniers, *La céramique chypriote de style figuré*, Rome 1974, (Biblioteca di antichità cipriote 2, Texte), 6 and 7, Fig. 2, and Supplément, XII and 1–2 (SA.1), Rome 1979, (Biblioteca di antichità cipriote 5).

The amphora, which is 40 cm high and belongs to class Proto-White Painted, is decorated with fishes, a ship and two human figures. The main motif is a shoal of fishes, and between two of them is a ship with two human figures roughly outlined in silhouette. The figures seem to have oars in their hands.

The amphora is of LC III date.

13. Graffito of a ship.
Fig. 13.
Provenance: Enkomi.
C.F.A. Schaeffer, *Enkomi-Alasia, Nouvelles missions en Chypre, 1946–1950,* Paris 1952, 102–103; Casson, 31, Fig. 27; Gray, G. 20, 52.

What is stern and what is bow of this ship is difficult to know. The curve of what could be a wind-blown sail indicates that the bow is the left part of the ship. On the other hand, if the three vertical lines are steering-oars the left end must be the stern. Even if the design is very simple, the engraver has succeeded in reproducing the essential feeling of a fast sailing-ship. This has also been mentioned by Schaeffer.

As this graffito has disappeared after the Turkish invasion, it is not possible to give a more detailed description.

The graffito is dated to 1200–1100 BC.

14. Graffiti of ships.
Fig. 14.
Provenance: Kition.
V. Karageorghis, *Kition,* London 1976, 99–100, Pl. 73 and 74; *BCH* 103, 1979, 698–700, Fig. 65–66; *BCH* 104, 1980, 783–785, Fig. 63; *AJA* 8, 1980, 66, Pl. 12, Fig. 19.

On the south façade of a temple building at Kition there are about fifteen graffiti of ships. This wall consists of eight ashlar blocks, each of them measuring roughly 150 x 300 cm. The graffiti are very roughly drawn and may be compared with graffiti on Malta and at Hyria. They are not yet published and cannot be described in more detail. D. Woolner 'Graffiti of ships at Tarxien, Malta', *Antiquity* 31, 1957, 60–67, Fig. 1–3, and C. Blegen, 'Hyria', *Hesperia,* Supplement VIII, Athens 1949, 39–42, Pl. 7.6.

15. Graffiti of ships.
Fig. 15.
Provenance: Kition.
V. Karageorghis, *Kition,* London 1976, 88–94, Pl. 68.

Stone anchors have been used in the construction of Temple 4 at Kition. Karageorghis suggests that from the beginning they may have been votive gifts. On two of the altar stones in this temple there are graffiti of ships. They are not yet published and cannot be described in more detail.

This temple and altar are dated around 1200 BC. ·

16. Cylinder with ship motif.
Fig. 16.
Cyprus Museum, Nicosia, Inv. No. N. 40.
Provenance: Further provenance in Cyprus unknown. It belongs to the Eustathios Constantinides Collection.
Dikaios, 115; *SCE* IV: 1D, 643, Fig. 86:42 and 647.

The cylinder shows two similar ships crewed by two human figures, one of them a helmsman with an oar. From the forked top of the mast, placed amidships, two parallel stays run to the top of each stem. Between the stems there are seven or eight parallel vertical lines running from gunwale to keel. These lines probably represent either the ribs of the hull or the number of oars.

The cylinder is dated to a late phase of LC.

C. CYPRO—GEOMETRIC PERIOD

17. Clay model of ship.
Fig. 17.
National Maritime Museum, Haifa.
Provenance: Further provenance in Cyprus unknown.
R.R. Stieglitz, 'An ancient terra-cotta ship from Cyprus', *Sefunim* IV (1972–1975), 44–46, Pl. VI, 3; Göttlicher, 31, No. 107, Pl. 7; M. – Ch. de Graeve, *The ships of the Ancient Near East (c. 2000–500 B.C.),* Leuven 1981, 124.
L.o.a. 18.5 cm.
Height amidships about 2 cm.

The model is undamaged. The clay is light beige and painted in bichrome technique. The hull is slim and elegant. One stem rises 3 cm above the gunwale and slants slightly inwards. The other rises vertically 3.5 cm above the gunwale with a protruding top, probably indicating some kind of head. The gunwale is uneven.

I should like to draw attention to an interesting detail. The lower part of the highest stem has been pinched together by the maker, thus creating a sharp curved cutwater. The painted decoration is composed of horizontal red and black stripes about 0.2 cm wide. At the bottom of the hull there is one irregular black stripe following the curve of the ship. Above this stripe, there is a red one following the gunwale and crossing the stems. The two stems are decorated with three sets of parallel bands: from the top, red, black and red. The last ones are connected with the red stripe along the gunwale, thus forming a continuous line between the stems.

The model is dated around the middle of the 11th century BC.

18. Cylindrical amphora decorated with a masted ship.
Fig. 18.
Cyprus Museum, Nicosia, Inv. No. B. 63.
Provenance: Curium.
Dikaios, 57, Pl. XI, 5; Gray, G. 21, 4.

The masted ship is highly stylized to fit into the geometrical design. From the top of the mast there are many wavy lines running down to the gunwale, probably stays.

The amphora is dated to Cypro-Geometric I.

D. CYPRO—ARCHAIC PERIOD

19. Clay model of ship.
Fig. 19.
Cyprus Museum, Nicosia, Inv. No. 1935 C. 57.
Provenance: Further provenance in Cyprus unknown.
Dikaios, 204; Göttlicher, 37, No. 171a, Pl. 12.
L.o.a. 31.5 cm.
Beam amidships 10 cm.
Height amidships 7 cm.

The wall is thin and smooth. The colour of the clay is light yellow-red, with dark painted decoration. The model is in good condition, except that a part of the aft body is missing and the forebody is slightly damaged. The ship has a socket amidships to hold a mast. There are eight holes through the gunwale. Four of them are placed aft, two and two. Two are placed immediately ahead of the mast on both sides and the last two about 3 cm from the stem. The keel strake is marked on the outside, ending in a kind of ram in the bow, not very clearly indicated.

The fore stem is painted with a cross-hatched pattern. Stems and keel strake are strongly marked with a dark painted line. Aft of the check decoration, about 3 cm below the gunwale there is a sharply defined horizontal line. The gunwale is also marked in the same way. Between these two lines there are sixteen oblique, parallel lines on the port side. On the same side there is also one single short line drawn vertically from the gunwale downwards, about 1.5 cm long and placed 6 cm aft of the fore stem. Aft of the last of the sixteen oblique lines, there is a part about 2 cm wide with a cross-hatched pattern vaguely indicated. Behind this pattern is a dark coloured part. As on the port side there are also on the starboard side two strongly defined lines with sixteen oblique parallel lines between. Aft of the last of these lines there is a triangle, 2.5 x 3.0 x 3.0 cm, in a lighter brown colour. Within the hull there are four dark transverse lines drawn from gunwale to gunwale, one 7 cm aft of the stem, one 7 cm further aft, one 7 cm still further aft and finally one 6 cm aft from this. Level with the second line there is a clearly marked mast-socket, painted dark.

Although not a parallel, it is interesting to compare the model described above with the clay model of a ship from Eridu mentioned among others by Casson p. 22 Fig. 20. It is dated to 3400 BC. There is no resemblance between the hulls, but the Eridu item has six holes in the hull, not three as Casson suggests, placed roughly in the same way. Perhaps the holes have been fastening points for stays and sheet-lines as well as for securing the cargo.

The model is of Cypro-Archaic date.

20. Clay model of ship.
Fig. 20.
Cyprus Museum, Nicosia, Inv. No. 1935 C. 56.
Provenance: Amathus.
Dikaios, 204; Göttlicher, 37, No. 171 b. Pl. 12.
L.o.a. 19 cm.
Beam amidships 6.5 cm.
Height amidships 3.5 cm.

The model is in good condition and only slightly damaged. It is elegantly made. The colour of the clay is red. Of the painted bichrome decoration there are now only faint traces visible. The prow is dolphin-shaped with an eye painted on both sides. There are no keel markings outside or inside the hull but afore there is a clearly marked ram. About 3 cm aft of the stem there is a thwart, 4 cm long, 1 cm wide and protruding 0.5 cm outside the hull on both sides. Aft, there is another thwart at the same distance from the stern stem, 4.5 cm long, 1 cm wide and protruding in the same way outside the hull. The end of the stern has no visible markings. There are eight oblique black lines on both sides of the hull. Between these lines there are eight vaguely marked similar red lines on one side and only two, but clearly marked, on the other side. Forward, below the protruding part of the thwart on the starboard side, there is an oval black decoration, 4 x 2 cm, the eye. The ram is marked with an almost vertical red line. The top part of the stem is missing. On the port side there is a similar oval marking below the protruding part of the fore thwart, 3.5 x 2 cm, with a strong vertical line in the middle.

Parallels to this model are especially two items, both from Amathus, Nos. 34 and 40 infra.

The model is of Cypro-Archaic date.

21. Clay model of ship.
Fig. 21.
Cyprus Museum, Nicosia, Inv. No. 1937/VI–8/3.
Provenance: Probably Yialousa.
Dikaios, 204; Gray, G. 31, 3.j).
L.o.a. 19 cm.
Beam amidships 5.5 cm.
Height amidships 3.5 cm.

The model is crudely made and slightly damaged. Although made in a very rough way no fingerprints can be seen. The bottom of the hull is flat with a rugged surface outside, while the interior has a smooth surface. The clay is yellow-red with traces of red-painted decoration on the outside. The ship has very few details, except the stem, which is formed like an animal's head with eyes and traces of incised grooves. The stems are clearly raised and the upper part of one stem is missing. The ship has a crew of two persons, one big and one small facing each other. These are made in "snow-man" technique, i.e. with topped caps and protruding noses, chins and ears. The big figure has both his arms outside the gunwale and holds an oar 6 cm long. According to Dikaios p. 204 there is one oarsman and one second seated figure, possibly the helmsman. On the other hand it could be suggested that the big figure might instead represent the helmsman holding the steering oar, and the small figure just a member of the crew. One reason for this suggestion is that the prows of the ships were often formed like animal's heads, and that the oar could be a steering oar as well as a rowing oar.

The model is of Cypro-Archaic date.

22. Clay model of ship.
Fig. 22.
Cyprus Museum, Nicosia.
Provenance: Salamis, *Cellarka,* Tomb 104, No. 5.
V. Karageorghis, *Salamis in Cyprus,* London 1969, 136, Pl. 79; Göttlicher, 35, No. 156, Pl. 10; V. Karageorghis, *Excavations in the necropolis of Salamis II,* London 1970, 149 and Pl. CLXXVI:5.
Length 11 cm.
The boat is crewed by a human figure. Karageorghis suggests that it is a rower. At any rate this item is made in such a primitive way, that the function of this figure is uncertain.
The model is dated to Cypro-Archaic I.

23. Clay model of ship.
Fig. 23.
Cyprus Museum, Nicosia, Inv. No. 1953/XII–30/6.
Provenance: Kalokhorio Klirou, *Zithkionas,* west of Politiko.
JHS 74, 1954, 174, Fig. 1; Casson, 69, note 124; Gray, G. 31, 3. i; Göttlicher, 36, No. 161, Pl. 11.
L.o.a. 30 cm.
Beam amidships 14 cm.
Height amidships 10 cm.
The model is slightly damaged but repaired, and there are only small fragments missing. The clay is red and its quality is coarse and rough. There is no other decoration than traces of red colour along gunwale and stems. The ship is rather clumsily made. Originally there have been three figures on board. The figure in the prow is now missing, lost in connection with exhibitions in Europe. The hull has a flattened bottom with a marked keel on the outside. Inside the hull there is no kelson or any frames indicated. The stems are raised about 6 cm above the gunwale. There are four thwarts, one 7 cm from the stem and then three at intervals of 4 cm. There is an aft deck about 7 cm from the stern frame. The front part of the deck is 10 cm wide and has a transverse bulkhead down to the stern thwart. In the middle of this bulkhead there is a quadrangular opening, 3.5 x 4.0 cm. Through the second thwart from aft there is a mast fastened in a socket in the floor. The existing mast is 8 cm long, 2.5 cm in diameter and ends in a crow's nest, 3.5 cm high and 3 cm in diameter. In this crow's nest one of the figures is placed. This figure is 7 cm high. He seems to be the look-out man. The helmsman, 8 cm high,

is sitting and holds in his right hand a strongly made, 13 cm long, steering oar. The blade of the oar is 4 cm wide; like that of the port oar it is thicker in the middle, becoming thinner towards the edges, and is shaped in the same way as a present-day oar. At 3 cm and 6 cm from the tip of the handle of this oar there are two strong ribbons about 1.5 cm wide, indicating the fastening to the hull. There is a similar steering-oar on the port side. Part of this oar, however, is missing and only 8 cm remain. The figures are made in the "snow-man" technique with topped caps and strongly marked noses, ears and chins. The quadrangular opening in the middle of the bulkhead is similar to the arrangements of the item No. 8 supra as well as of No. 32 infra.

The model is of Cypro-Archaic II date.

24. Clay model of ship.
Fig. 24.
Cyprus Museum, Nicosia.
Provenance: Amathus, Tomb 3, No. 23.
BCH 101, 1977, 765–766, Fig. 98.
L.o.a. 20 cm.
Beam amidships 6 cm.
Height amidships 3 cm.

The clay model is damaged, broken in two pieces but complete. The colour of the clay is yellow-red, with bichrome decoration in black and red. The ship is long and slender with an unusual, concave freeboard and a rounded bottom below the waterline. One of the stems is slightly curved upwards. The bow one is in the form of an animal's head. Near both ends of the ship there is a cross-beam or thwart resting on the gunwale and slightly protruding on both sides of the hull. The bow one is 3 cm long and 0.5 cm wide, the stern one 4.5 cm long and 1 cm wide. At the water-line the bow has a pointed ram, sloping slightly downwards. On the port side, 2 cm aft of the point of the ram, there is an oval eye, 2 cm long and 1 cm high, with a big pupil painted in black. Very faint traces of a similar decoration can be seen on the starboard side. The concave freeboard is 1.5 cm high and painted black between the cross-beams. The gunwale, the cross-beams, and the upper edge of the ram, as well as the upper parts of the stems, are painted red. The model has no interior fittings.

It is of Cypro-Archaic date.

There is another clay model of a ship from recent excavations at Amathus, which is only mentioned in *BCH* 101, 1977, 766.

25. *Clay model of ship.*
Fig. 25.
Cyprus Museum, Nicosia, Inv. No. 1956 X–1/1 M.
Provenance: Lysi, Famagusta district.
L.o.a. 18 cm.
Beam amidships 3.5 cm.
Height amidships 2.5 cm.

The shape of the hull is long and slender. The stems are canoe-shaped and strongly marked. One of them is damaged. This one protrudes 1 cm and the undamaged one 2.5 cm upwards above the gunwale. The colour of the clay is red, slightly darker on the outside of the hull. There is no painted decoration. In the clay on both sides of the model there are faint vertical and parallel contour lines. One hypothesis is that these markings might indicate quite another method of shipbuilding technique, namely hide stretched upon wooden frames, a method known from the Euphrates and the Tigris. Interesting as this hypothesis may be the simple explanation is probably that these markings are only fingerprints from the making of the model.

The model is of Cypro-Archaic date.

26. *Clay model of ship.*
Fig. 26.
Cyprus Museum, Nicosia, Inv. No. 1946/XII–23/1.
Provenance: Further provenance in Cyprus unknown.
Göttlicher, 36, No. 159, Pl. 10.
L.o.a. 18 cm.
Beam amidships 4.5 cm.
Height amidships 2.5 cm.

The model is slender and made of smooth, light-coloured clay painted in bichrome. The colour is now faded. The axe-shaped stems are raised 4.5 cm above the gunwale. The stems are red-painted, except the upper parts. The gunwale all along the ship is marked with an uneven, red-painted ribbon about 1.5 cm wide. The lower part of the hull has faintly visible traces of black colour. There are three human figures and one animal in the boat. The figures are made in the "snow-man" technique, have their arms resting on the gunwale and are looking in the same direction. Their eyes are clearly marked in black. Their clothes are clearly indicated by black lines on the sleeves. The animal may be a dog or a sheep. Behind the animal, whose back part is slightly damaged, there is a fragment amidships of what could have been a mast-socket. On both sides of this socket there are other small fragments, probably of two belaying-pins.

Inside the hull, there are red lines drawn from gunwale to gunwale, even across the feet of the figures. These lines must represent frames. There are three frames at intervals of 4 cm. There are no thwarts or keel markings inside, and the figures seem to be placed directly on the floor.

The model is of Cypro-Archaic date.

27. *Clay model of ship.*
Fig. 27.
Famagusta Museum, Famagusta, Inv. No. 1933/IX–13/2.
Provenance: Further provenance in Cyprus unknown.
According to Dr. Kyriakos Nicolaou, there are reasons for believing that it has been found in the vicinity of Famagusta, as the model was placed in the Famagusta Museum.
L.o.a. 12.5 cm.
Beam amidships 3 cm.
Height 4.5 cm.

The boat is hand-made and undamaged. It is rather roughly made and lacks details. There are no fingerprints. The clay is of rough quality and red in colour with bichrome decoration. The boat is crewed by two boatsmen, one in the bow and one in the stern, facing each other. They are roughly made, and somewhat difficult to distinguish from the hull of the boat. Their arms are resting on the gunwale. There is no indication of their sex. There are no other interior fittings. The hull is decorated with red and black stripes outside and black ones inside. The width of these stripes is 0.6 cm, 0.5 cm and 0.3 cm. The stripes are vertical, parallel and running from the gunwale to the bottom of the boat. Some of the stripes are uneven and only faint traces of them are visible. Although the models are not parallels, certain details are similar to those of the item No. 49 infra.

The model is of Cypro-Archaic date.

28. *Clay model of ship.*
Fig. 28.
Pierides Collection, Larnaca.
Provenance: Further provenance in Cyprus unknown.
P. Åström, 'Cypern – en kulturhistorisk och konsthistorisk skiss' in *Cypern – motsättningarns ö,* Gothenburg 1974, (*SIMA* Pocket-book 1), 33, 79.

L.o.a. 14 cm.

Beam amidships 4 cm.

Height amidships 4 cm.

The model is hand-made and undamaged. The clay is rather rough and the colour is buff. There are faint traces of decoration painted in red and black. The hull is canoe-shaped with a rounded bottom and distinctly marked stems. The gunwale is uneven. There are two roughly modelled human figures, about 6 cm high, sitting with their backs towards each stem. Figures and hull, however, intermingle and there is no clear distinction. The arms of the figures are resting on the gunwale. The lower parts of the bodies are flattened against the hull, and there is no indication of their sex. There are no other interior fittings. The painted decoration is composed of irregular horizontal red and black stripes about 0.4–0.6 cm wide. At the bottom of the outside of the hull there is a red stripe, then a black, a red, and at last a black one following the gunwale. The decoration is similar on both sides of the hull. On one of the stems there are two parallel, oblique lines in black, 0.2 cm wide and 2 cm long. The figure above this last oblique decoration has a black-painted eye.

The model is of Cypro-Archaic I date.

29. Clay model of ship.

Fig. 29.

Pierides Collection, Larnaca.

Provenance: Further provenance in Cyprus unknown.

L.o.a. 12 cm.

Beam amidships 4.5 cm.

Height amidships 2.5 cm,

The model is hand-made, slightly damaged and has black painted decoration. The clay is grey with an admixture of white, and rather rough. The model is made in a clumsy way, the shape is warped and the gunwale uneven. The interior, on the other hand is smoother. The hull is canoe-shaped and the stems are distinctly marked. The bottom is flattened. There are no interior fittings. On both sides of the exterior of the hull there are faint traces of painted decoration in a net pattern. Both the stems are curved upwards, one of them with a prolonged part pointing inwards and slightly warped. The unusual shape may indicate that the maker intended to form a human figure. But if such is the case he has not carried through this intention. It ought to be mentioned that this stem has been mended and its rather bizarre shape may cast certain doubts on

the correctness of this restoration.
The model is of Cypro-Archaic date.

30. Clay model of ship.
Fig. 30.
Pierides Collection, Larnaca.
Provenance: Further provenance in Cyprus unknown.
P. Åström, 'Cypern – en kulturhistorisk och konsthistorisk skiss' in *Cypern – motsättningarnas ö,* Gothenburg 1974, (*SIMA* Pocket-book 1), 33, 79.
L.o.a. 8.5 cm.
Beam amidships 3.5 cm.
Height amidships 2.5 cm.
Height from bottom to top of stem 4 cm.
    The model is hand-made. The clay is red in colour, with dark brown and black painted decoration. The hull is canoe-shaped. The middle part of the bottom of the hull is flat. The gunwale is uneven. One of the stems projects upwards 1.5 cm. On the lower part of this stem, as a prolongation of the water-line, there is a protruding ram. The painted decoration of the hull is very faint and seems to be similar on both sides. On each side of the stem immediately aft of the ram there is a black oval-shaped eye, 1.5 x 1 cm, with a black pupil. The combination of eye and ram at one end of the ship indicates that this must be the bow. Just below the gunwale there are two parallel, horizontal red lines about 0.3 cm wide. At the prow on the starboard side there are, furthermore, two oblique, black lines running from the gunwale downwards. These lines may represent oars. Aft, there are two black lines running vertically from the gunwale downwards. The decoration on the port side is roughly similar, although there is only one black vertical line aft. On the port side there are also traces of black colour on the projecting stem. A parallel to this item is No. 37 infra.
    The model is of Cypro-Archaic I date.

31. Clay model of ship.
Fig. 31.
British Museum, London, Inv. No. 94. 11–1. 282.
Provenance: Amathus, Tomb 73 (Turner Bequest Excavations).
CT, 35, A 204; Murray, 112, Fig. 164, 17; Gray, G. 31, 3 f, Pl. G. IV c, e; (The last ref. Pl. G. IV *e* is due to a mistake by Gray – should be Pl. G. IV *d.*) Göttlicher, 36 No. 165, Pl. 10 and Pl. 12.

L.o.a. 17.5 cm.

Beam amidships 7.2 cm.

Height amidships 3.2 cm.

The stems project 5.7 cm above the gunwale. The model is damaged and part of the hull is missing. The clay is buff in colour, with painted decoration in bichrome. The gunwale is red with horizontal black and red lines below. The tips of the stems are painted red. Near each stem there is a thwart or cross-beam. Amidships inside the ship there is a mast-socket.

The model is of Cypro-Archaic date.

By courtesy of Mr. D.M. Bailey of the British Museum, I have received an extract of the excavation report concerning Tomb 73, which reads as follows:

"No 73. Terracotta horse
                    bird
                    boat."

This report does not help in dating the model.

32. Clay model of ship.

Fig. 32.

British Museum, London, Inv. No. 94.11–1182.

Provenance: Amathus, Tomb 83 (Turner Bequest Excavations).

CT, 35, A 202; Murray, 112 and 119, Fig. 164, 12; R.D. Barnett, 'Early shipping in the Near East in Antiquity', *Antiquity* 32, 1958, 227, Pl. XXIV; M. Bonino, 'Un modello di nave cipriota del sec. VI–V a. C.', *Rivista di Studi Liguri* 31, 1965, 301–310; B. Landström, *Sailing ships,* London 1969, 27; Gray, G. 31, 3.d), Pl. G. III a–c; Casson, 65–66, 69, Figs. 86–87; Göttlicher, 35, No. 153, Pl. 10 with further references.

L.o.a. 31 cm.

Beam amidships 9 cm.

Height amidships 7 cm.

The stern part rises about 3.5 cm above the gunwale. The model is rather coarsely made and slightly damaged. The clay is thin and red-brown, with bichrome decoration. There is a black line about 1.5 cm wide running from the stern shaft to a cathead. The rest of the hull shows uneven faint traces of a colour decoration (Murray, p. 112, however, has described the ship as brilliantly painted in yellow and black upon the red colour of the clay). According to Bonino there should be the classical eye-motif on each side of the bow. Personally, I did not observe any such traces. As there has been an interval of ten years between our observations, this decoration may now have faded away. Inside the ship there are black dots on the cross-beams and on the beams on either side of the mast-socket. According to the excavation report and to Murray p. 112 there has been an iron steering paddle attached to the shaft on the port side, which is now missing. Murray also suggests p. 112 that some object, perhaps a human figure, is missing from the second thwart. This ship is a most interesting and detailed example of shipbuilding and seems to give a realistic picture of a contemporary type of ship. The hull is heavy and has a rounded bottom. There is a pronounced tumble-home, i.e. the beam at the water-line or half way above the water-line is wider than at gunwale level. The model has an elevated poop-deck, connected on each side of the hull with two vertical partly open shafts, attached to the outside of the hull. The poop-deck has bulwarks towards the outside of the ship but is open forwards. The length of the poop-deck is about a quarter the length of the ship. On each side of the poop-deck there is a round hole downwards, connected with the vertical shafts on the outside of the hull.

I entirely agree with Bonino p. 304, Fig. 4, in his reconstruction of these shafts as holders of the steering oars. The above-mentioned iron oar confirms this interpretation. In the middle of the poop-deck there is a rectangular hole through which a similar lower deck could be reached. This lower deck may have served as quarters for the crew. The poop-deck is supported by two short pillars from the lower deck. This part of the ship, consequently, must have been used for navigation, manoeuvring and quarters. The remaining three-quarters of the ship probably served as cargo space. Inside the ship there is a dark line indicating the keel. In the middle of the interior there is a cross-beam arrangement surrounding a mast-socket. Fore and aft there is another cross-beam, each painted with black dots. A small cross-beam at the bow is connected with two cuts one on each side in the gunwale, and certainly served to fasten the painter or the anchor line. Just below this cut there is, on each side, traces of what ought to have been catheads for the anchors. From the lower part of the steering shaft running forwards there is a somewhat uneven row of holes of irregular sizes. On both sides of the ship the middle hole is about twice as big as the others. As these holes are placed slightly above the level of the interior cross-beams, this may indicate that a lower inner deck has existed and that the holes may have served as scuppers. This hypothesis is supported by Bonino p. 304. Another reason to believe that the row of holes ought to represent scuppers in the fact that the middle hole, where most water is drained, is the largest one. On the other hand, as all merchant ships in this part of the Mediterranean had to rely on oars for a speedy delivery of goods, such a row of holes often indicated oar-holes. The mast-socket proves that it must have been a sailing ship. Consequently the black dots on the interior beams must be considered as fastening points for stays as well as sheet-lines. There has probably been only one big square sail carried by a yard. Among the reasons for the pronounced tumble-home of the hull could be mentioned

    a) a lowering of the centre of gravity to acquire a steadying effect,

    b) to get a larger and more sheltered space for the cargo,

    c) to create a flatter hull with less draught to enable the ship to enter shallower waters.

According to Barnett p. 227 this type of ship was called a golah. This ship model has much in common with the clay model from the private collection of Mr. Nicos Kirzis, which is dated to the Late Cypriote period. Their similarities include such features as the poop-deck, the tumble-home of the hull and the row of holes. Although the ship from the Nicos Kirzis Collection is of much earlier date and certain details are not as pronounced compared with the ship described above, it clearly shows that even at this early date shipbuilding had already been brought to a high technical level.

The model is of Cypro-Archaic date. According to Gray a more exact dating than the 7th century BC is uncertain. Casson, however, dates the ship to the 9th or 8th century BC and Göttlicher to 800 BC.

By courtesy of Mr. D.M. Bailey of the British Museum I have received an extract of the excavation report concerning Tomb 83, which reads as follows:

"Jan 10, 1894 B No 83

Small cave 6 ft 6 in from back to front, 8 ft 6 in wide shaft 12 feet deep. Doorway of three stones, closed with a large slab at the door. Four bodies were lying along on the left, and two on the right. The tomb had not been robbed, but for the later interments some of the objects had been heaped up in the corners. The terracottas were lying in a mass, on the middle of the right side, close to the wall.

Contents. Glass, alabaster,

Terracotta boat, 13 in long with poop, and iron steering paddle 2 smaller boats

Terracotta fig in shrine surmounted by Uraei

Terracotta head wearing crown of Upper Egypt with Uraeus

Terracotta Kriophoros, bearded, painted
Terracotta fem. fig. rude type
Terracotta birds bell
Terracotta horses
Terracotta horseman
Terracotta horse and chariot
Terracotta wine cart (?)
Terracotta large satyric mask
b.f. lekythus, warriors fighting and spectators
b.f. kylix– fragts
2 small Egyptian eyes (porcelain)
Electrum ear-ring
Glass beads, etc. – Bronze settings
Silver bracelet
1 pair gold earrings with pendants."

It is consequently evident that this excavation report, which is very sketchy, does not contribute much to a closer analysis of the dating of this ship. Personally I would date the model to the sixth century BC having regard to the black-figured items in the tomb.

33. Clay model of ship.
Fig. 33.
British Museum, London, Inv. No. 94.11–1 183.
Provenance: Amathus, Tomb 83 (Turner Bequest Excavations).
CT, 35, A 203; Murray, 113, Fig. 164, 19; Gray, G. 31, 3. e), Pl.
G. IV d; (The last ref. Pl. G. IV *d* is due to a mistake by Gray – should be Pl. G. IV *e.)* Göttlicher, 37, No. 170, Pl. 12.
L.o.a. 21 cm.
Beam amidships 7 cm.
Height amidships 5 cm.

The stems project 3 and 4 cm respectively above the gunwale. The model is damaged. The clay is reddish in colour and faint traces of painted decoration can be detected on the outside of the hull. According to Murray, p. 113, fig. 164, 19, two parallel oblique lines can be seen on one of the stems, and the ship was also painted within. The colour of the stripes were red, yellow and red. This design, however, now seems to have disappeared.

The clay is thick and rather rough. Longitudinal stripes along the sides of the hull may indicate the manner of building. The upper ends of the stems are formed like fish-tails. Amidships inside the hull there is a mast-socket about 2.0 x 1.5 cm. 2 cm from one of the stems there is a transverse beam 4.5 cm long and 0.5 cm thick, placed on the gunwale and slightly protruding outside the hull. About 1 cm below the gunwale, between the stem and the transverse beam, there is a hole through the hull. This hole may be compared with the cuts in the gunwale on No. 32 supra, and would consequently have been intended for the painter or the anchor-line fastened to the cross-beam.

I would date the model to the sixth century BC. See further No. 32 supra.

34. Clay model of ship.
Fig. 34.
British Museum, London, Inv. No. 94.11–1184.
Provenance: Amathus, Tomb 83 (Turner Bequest Excavations).
CT, 36, A 208; Murray, 112, Fig. 164, 10; Gray, G. 31, 3. e); Göttlicher, 38, No. 173, Pl. 13.
L.o.a. 17 cm.
Beam amidships 3.8 cm.
Height amidships 2.5 cm.

The stems project 3 cm above the gunwale. The model is roughly made and is slightly damaged. The colour of the clay is buff. The hull has painted decoration in red, black and yellow colours. There are no interior fittings. Even if the model is roughly made the lines of the hull are slender and elegant. The ship is decorated both inside and outside the hull. Inside there is a black line about 1 cm wide along the keel and following the stems upwards. Along both sides just below the gunwale, there is a red line about 1 cm wide from stem to stem. The exterior of the ship is decorated with longitudinal stripes, black, red, black and yellow from the gunwale down. The yellow stripe is 1 cm wide and the others about 0.5 cm. Both the stems have traces of a yellow decoration.

Like the other clay models of ships from Tomb 83, I would date this one to the sixth century BC.

35. Clay model of ship.
Fig. 35.
British Museum, London, No. 94.11–1185.
Provenance: Amathus, Tomb 83 (Turner Bequest Excavations).
CT, 35, A 205; Murray, 112, Fig. 164, 16; Gray, G. 31, 3 e), Pl. G. IV b; Göttlicher, 36, No. 160, Pl. 10.
L.o.a. 15.5 cm.

Beam amidships 4.5 cm.
Height amidships 3.5 cm.

From the stem 6.5 cm forwards on one side, the bulwark projects 1.5 cm above the rest of the gunwale. This elevated part probably indicates a poop-deck. The height from the keel to the top of both stems is 6.5 cm. The model is slightly damaged and parts of the bulwark and the gunwale on one side are missing. The clay is smooth and the model is made in an elegant manner. The bottom of the hull is rounded. The ship has no interior decoration or equipment. The colour of the clay is buff. The outside of the hull is decorated with horizontal painted stripes in red and black. The undamaged side of the hull is covered with stripes in bichrome technique, three on the lower part of the hull and five on the part with the elevated bulwark. The stripes are about 0.5 to 1 cm wide. The decoration on the other side of the hull seems to have been similar, although part of the hull is missing. One of the stems is decorated with two parallel red bands.

The model is of Cypro-Archaic date. See further No. 32 supra.

36. *Clay model of ship.*
Fig. 36.
British Museum, London, Inv. No. 94.11–1186.
Provenance: Amathus, Tomb 83 (Turner Bequest Excavations).
CT, 36, A 209; Murray, 113, Fig. 164, 20; Gray, G. 31, 3. e); Göttlicher, 38, No. 174, Pl. 13.
L.o.a. 13 cm.
Beam amidships 4.5 cm.
Height amidships 3.5 cm.

The stems project 2 cm and 2.5 cm respectively above the gunwale. One side of the gunwale is damaged. The clay is smooth with a reddish colour. The outside of the hull is decorated with longitudinal stripes in bichrome technique. The hull is slender with a rounded bottom. There is nothing to indicate by what means this ship was propelled. The ship is decorated in the same manner on both sides. The design consists of two horizontal parallel bands about 1 cm wide, the upper one red and the lower one black, following the sheer of the hull from stem to stem. There are also traces of a black band along the gunwale. The stems are decorated with one red and one black band, somewhat thinner than the bands along the hull. These bands are horizontal and parallel.

The model is of Cypro-Archaic date. See further No. 32 supra.

37. Clay model of ship.
Fig. 37.
British Museum, London, Inv. No. 94.11–1187.
Provenance: Amathus, Tomb 83 (Turner Bequest Excavations).
CT, 36, A 210; Murray, 113, Fig. 164, 18; Gray, G. 31, 3. e); Göttlicher,
38, No. 175, Pl. 12.
L.o.a. 8 cm.
Beam amidships 4 cm.
Height amidships 2 cm.
Height from bottom to top of undamaged stem 4 cm and to top of
damaged stem 3 cm. The model is small and tubby and partly damaged.
The colour of the clay is yellow-red with painted red-brown design. The
bottom of the hull is rounded and the gunwale unevenly formed. Between the rounded bottom and the vertical freeboard with its slight
tumble-home there is a marked transition. Immediately inside the undamaged stem there is a transverse beam 4 cm long and 1 cm wide,
placed on the gunwale and slightly protruding outside the hull. At the
water-line the undamaged stem ends in a small, rounded ram. The hull is
decorated on one side with seven oblique lines in red-brown colour from
the gunwale downwards. The design on the other side of the hull is
similar but more obscure. There is a parallel to this item among the clay
models of the Pierides Collection in Larnaca.
The model is of Cypro-Archaic date. See further No. 32 supra.

38. Fragment of a clay model of ship.
Fig. 38.
British Museum, London, Inv. No. 94.11–1188.
Provenance: Amathus, Tomb 83 (Turner Bequest Excavations).
CT, 36, A 211; Murray, 113, Fig. 164, 24; Gray, G. 31, 3. e); Göttlicher,
38, No. 176, Pl. 13.
Length 9 cm.
Height 9 cm.
The clay is reddish in colour and unpainted. The item is smoothly
modelled. There are some interesting details. Just below the gunwale,
1.5 cm, there is a horizontal protection planking 1.5 cm broad running in
two parallel bands all the way round the stem. 4 cm from the fore-part of
the stem there is a piece protruding 1.5 cm from the upper part of the
protection planking. This probably represents a cathead, a piece projecting from the bow, to which the anchor was secured.
The item is of Cypro-Archaic date. See further No. 32 supra.

39. Clay model of ship.
Fig. 39.
British Museum, London, Inv. No. 94.11–1258.
Provenance: Amathus, Tomb 88 (Turner Bequest Excavations).
CT, 36, A 207; Murray, 114, Fig. 165, 6; Gray, G. 31, 3. g); Göttlicher,
37, No. 168, Pl. 12.
L.o.a. 15.8 cm.
Beam amidships 3.7 cm.
Height amidships 3 cm.

The colour of the clay is orange-buff, with painted bichrome decoration. The stems rise 1 cm above the gunwale. The stern stem is pointed and curved inwards. The water-line is marked by a black line about 0.2 cm wide. Between this line and the gunwale on both sides of the hull there are red and black parallel, oblique lines. The first ten probably represent oars and the last one, which is slightly apart from the others and more horizontal, may be the steering-oar. There are also one black and one red line around the stern post. On each side of the bow, there is an eye with pupil and eyebrow painted in black. The bow stem projects slightly forwards at the water-line in a ram-like way. There are no interior fittings.

The model is of Cypro-Archaic date. By courtesy of Mr. D.M. Bailey of the British Museum I have received an extract of the excavation report concerning Tomb 88, which reads as follows:

"Jan 12, 1894. B. No. 88. Square cave about 9 x 9 feet, 10 feet below surface. Several bodies lying round the three sides on. . .
7 gold diadems, with palmette patterns
1 small ditto
1 pair gold earrings
1 small gold ring
         spirals ring

Silver bangles
         leaf
Bronze 4 bangles
         3 mirror
         spatula
         disk
         pin
Iron strigil

Terracotta 2 chariots
   2 boats
   4 birds
   Egyptian Bes
   Egyptian dwarf
   horseman
Porcelain Head of Bes small Egyptian figure
   glass gem"
 The excavation report does not contribute to a closer dating of this ship.

40. Clay model of ship.
Fig. 40.
British Museum, London, Inv. No. 94.11–1184 (517).
Provenance: Amathus, Tomb 176 (Turner Bequest Excavations).
CT, 35–36, A 206; Murray, 113, Fig. 164, 22; Gray, G. 31, 3 e); Göttlicher, 37–38, No. 172, Pl. 13.
L.o.a. 18 cm.
Beam amidships 4.5 cm.
Height amidships 3 cm.
 Height from bottom to top of the fore stem 5 cm. Height from bottom to top of the damaged stern stem 4 cm. The model is hand-made and has traces of fingerprints inside the hull. The clay is grey and rather thick. The bottom of the hull is flat and there are no interior fittings. The decoration is black and yellow. About 1 cm below the gunwale there is a horizontal black, somewhat uneven, broken line, interrupted 3 cm aft of the fore stem by two black vertical, parallel lines from gunwale to bottom. Even if similar lines on other ships have represented steering-oars, in this case I feel inclined to regard them as mere decoration, as other details mark this part of the ship as the bow. From these two vertical lines there is one broader and one finer black line running along the water-line towards the stern and following the stern stem upwards. Between the broad black line along the gunwale and the finer line along the water-line there is an undulating yellow line between the stern stem and the two vertical lines. This undulating line may have been somewhat more elaborate but is now only faintly indicated. The fore stem is decorated with a black eye, 2.5 cm long and 1.5 cm high, above which there is a horizontal eyebrow. In front of the eye there is a faintly oblique, vertical line. The snout-shaped ram is painted black. The fore stem also has very faint traces of a yellow decor. The two sides of the hull

are similarly decorated, although the decoration on the starboard side is more distinct.

The model is of Cypro-Archaic date. From the details in the excavation report a closer analysis of the date is not possible. An extract from this report concerning Tomb 176 reads as follows:

"Tomb 176
Cave about 7 ft down: entered through roof.
1 clay boat.
1 small-handled amphora
1 small shoulder-ray jug
1 cow
fragments of bronze
1 Sq. -porcelain ornament (1 cocked hat – some common jugs)".

41. Clay model of ship.
Fig. 41.
British Museum, London, Inv. No. 1938/11–30.6.
Provenance: Further provenance in Cyprus unknown.
Gray, G. 31, 3. h), Pl. G. IV a; Göttlicher, 35, No. 152 a, Pl. 10.
L.o.a. 17 cm.
Beam amidships 5 cm.
Height amidships 3 cm.

The colour of the clay is buff, and there is painted decoration in bichrome. The hull has a flat but slightly rounded bottom and a pronounced tumble-home. The model is slightly damaged, with the top of the stern stem missing. The shape and the decoration are in many ways similar to those of item No. 40 supra with the black lines, the eye and the snout-like ram. One difference is that the undulating line is more zigzag-like, more distinct and red-coloured. The ship has no interior fittings.

The model is of Cypro-Archaic date.

42. Part of clay model of ship.
Fig. 42.
British Museum, London, Inv. No. 94.11–1290.
Provenance: Amathus, Tomb 95 (Turner Bequest Excavations).
CT, 36, A 212; Göttlicher, 37, No. 171, Pl. 12.
Length 14.3 cm.
Height from keel to top of stem 9 cm.

The clay is grey and the hull rather thin, and there is no decoration. As on No. 43 infra the stem is forked. These two fragments are not joining.

There is a ram and also a thwart 2 cm from the stem. This thwart is 4 cm long and 1.5 cm wide.

The piece is dated to Cypro-Archaic times. An extract from the excavation report concerning Tomb 95 reads as follows:

"Jan 16, 1894. B No. 95.

Small roughly hewn cave opening into a shaft. the cave was very full of earth which seemed to have been sifted in heaps in the tomb.

Gold – small earring with globular pendant.

Bronze – 2 coins

Iron – strigil

Pottery – Many fragts of blackglazed ware + 1 saucer. Fragments of b.f. "oinochoë" with stamped subject in panel very fragmentary – al. Odysseus under arm advancing to r. –on r. Cyclops recumbent with club in l. hand r. hand extended. Plain red glazed ware Kantharos with roughly painted flowers.

Terracotta – Bows of boat, with ram.

Small fem. fig. standing early type.

Rude bearded mask with holes for suspension.

Limestone – small piedestal

Cone – as of thyrsus?

Recumbent fig. on couch. Traces of faint glass Roman

Fragments of variegated amphorae

Alabaster Amphora (one handle broken)

Alabastron

Sard beads etc"

Göttlicher dates this item to 600 BC. Personally I would date the model to the sixth century BC having regard to the black-figured fragments in the tomb.

43. Part of clay model of ship.
Fig. 43.
British Museum, London, Inv. No. 94.11–1291.
Provenance: Amathus, Tomb 95 (Turner Bequest Excavations).
CT, 36, A 213; Göttlicher, 37, No. 169, Pl. 12.
Length 11 cm.
Height from bottom to top of stem 10 cm.

The clay is grey and there is no decoration. The stem is forked and the shape similar to that of item No. 42 supra. 3 cm from the stem there is a thwart, 5 cm long and 1.5 cm wide, placed on the gunwale and slightly protruding outside the hull.

The piece is dated to Cypro-Archaic times. Göttlicher dates this item to 600 BC. I myself would date it to the sixth century BC. See further No. 42 supra.

44. Part of clay model of ship.
Fig. 44.
British Museum, London, Inv. No. 1967/11–329.
Provenance: Salamis (Cyprus Exploration Fund Excavations, circa 1890).
Length 7 cm.
The clay is grey and coarse. It is unpainted. There is a roughly modelled human figure sitting with his back towards the stem with the left arm resting on the gunwale. The lower part of the body is flattened against the hull. The figure is about 6 cm long. Although it is clumsily made, it seems to be made in the "snow-man" technique with topped cap and a strongly marked nose.
The piece is dated to the Cypro-Archaic period.

45. Clay model of ship.
Fig. 45.
Narodowe Museum, Cracow, Inv. No. XI–1236.
Provenance: Although the provenance is not known, a similarity to other items indicates a Cypriote origin. It was a gift from Prince Wladyslaw Czartoryski who sent it from Paris in 1893.
Z.J. Kapera, 'Terakotowy model barki morskiej', *Rozprawy i Sprawozdania Muzeum Narodowego w Krakowie* 10, Cracow 1970, 39–51, Figs. 47–49; Göttlicher, 36, No. 164, Pl. 11; Z.J. Kapera, 'Terakotowa flota Kinyrasa', *Bibliotheca Classica Orientalis 14,* Berlin 1969, 45–46.
L.o.a. 16.7 cm.
Beam amidships 6.2 cm.
Height amidships 5.5 cm.
The model is hand-made and damaged. The clay is light brown and mixed with fragments of white stone. The hull is bulgy, with a flat bottom in the middle part. The two stems project above the gunwale, and one of them is distinctly curved inwards the hull. This stem is slightly fish-tail-shaped while the other is pointed and more slender. The ship has no interior fittings, nor any indication of the means by which it was propelled. The model is painted in black and brown-red. One side of the hull has three horizontal stripes, black below the gunwale and near the bottom, and red between. The maximum width of the stripes is (from the

top) 0.6 cm, 0.5 cm and 0.3 cm respectively. There are only faint traces of the same decoration on the other side of the hull.

The ship lacks provenance, but many of its features are so similar to those of the Amathus ships, especially item No. 35 supra, that one may presume that the ship is of Cypriote origin. This is also the opinion of Kapera.

I would date the model to the Cypro-Archaic period.

46. Clay model of ship.
Fig. 46.
Narodowe Museum, Cracow, Inv. No. XI–1237.
Provenance: Although the provenance is not known, a similarity to other items indicates a Cypriote origin. Like No. 45 supra, it belongs to the Czartoryski Collection.
Z.J. Kapera, 'Terakatowy model barki morskiej', *Rozprawy i Sprawoz-dania Muzeum Narodowego w Krakowie 10,* Cracow 1970, 51; Gött-licher, 36, No. 158, Pl. 10; Z.J. Kapera, 'Terakotowa flota Kinyrasa', *Bibliotheca Classica Orientalis 14,* Berlin 1969, 45–46.
L.o.a. 12.3 cm.
Beam amidships 4.2 cm.

The model is damaged, with an uneven gunwale. There are no interior fittings. The stern is extended and crescent-shaped. The prow has a ram.

I would date the model to the Cypro-Archaic period.

47. Drawing of a clay model of ship.
Fig. 47.
Castle Goluchów, Cracow.
Göttlicher, 37, No. 166, Pl. 12; Z.J Kapera, 'Terakotowa flota Kiny-rasa', *Bibliotheca Classica Orientalis 14,* Berlin 1969, 45–46.

The original model was lost during the Second World War. It is believed that it was found at Amathus.

Available data come from a drawing made by W. Werner after an older drawing. The ram and the decoration along the gunwale show the same characteristics as No. 19 supra. According to traditions, there should have been an animal with four legs inside.

I consider the dating to be Cypro-Archaic.

48. Clay model of ship.
Fig. 48.
Kunsthistorisches Museum, Wien, Inv. No. V 1501.

Provenance: Amathus. Purchased by M. Ohnefalsch-Richter 1890.
AA 1892, 116, No. 110; M. Ohnefalsch-Richter, *Kypros, die Bibel und Homer,* Berlin 1893, Pl. CXLV, 6; Göttlicher, 36, No. 163, Pl. 11.
L.o.a. 28.3 cm.
Beam amidships 8.7 cm.
Height amidships 9.1 cm.
The model is hand-made in a rather coarse way. It is damaged. Part of the bow is missing. The colour of the clay is red. Amidships inside the hull there is a mast-socket. A string of clay along the gunwale towards one of the stems could indicate some kind of reinforcement.
  The model is of Cypro-Archaic date.

49. Clay model of ship.
Fig. 49.
Archaeological Museum, Istanbul, Inv. No. 5793.
Provenance: Further provenance in Cyprus unknown.
L.o.a. 12.5 cm.
Beam amidships about 4 cm.
Height amidships 4.5 cm.
Height from bottom to top of the high stem 7.5 cm.
The other stem is damaged.
  The clay is grey, rough and unpainted. The model is damaged but partly mended. One stem is missing above the gunwale. The bottom of the hull is flat and there are no interior fittings. The undamaged stem projects about 3 cm above the gunwale and is curved inwards. The damaged stem has a rounded ram protruding 2.5 cm from it. There is a roughly modelled human figure sitting with his back towards the undamaged stem and with his arms resting on the gunwale. The top of the head seems to be missing, and the lower part of the body is flattened against the hull. There is no indication of the sex of the figure. The model can be compared with Nos. 27 and 44 supra. The shape of the model as well as the material has much in common with these items, although there are two figures in No. 27.
  The model seems to be of Cypro-Archaic date.

50. Clay model of ship.
Fig. 50.
Metropolitan Museum of Art, New York, from the Cesnola Collection, Inv. No. 74.51. 1752.
Provenance: Amathus.

L.P. di Cesnola, *A descriptive Atlas of the Cesnola Collection of Cypriote Antiquities in the Metropolitan Museum of Art in New York, II,* Boston 1885, Pl. LXXVII No. 702; J.L. Myres, *Handbook of the Cesnola Collection of Antiquities from Cyprus,* New York 1914, 348; M. Ohnefalsch-Richter, *Kypros, die Bibel und Homer,* Berlin 1893, Pl. CXLV, 4; B. Landström, *Sailing ships,* London 1969, 27; Casson, 66–67, Fig. 94; Göttlicher, 36, No. 162, Pl. 11.

L.o.a. 25.7 cm.

Height amidships 10.7 cm.

The hull is rounded and skilfully modelled. It has faint traces of colour. The bottom of it is rounded, but the keel is more distinctly marked than on any other item hitherto described. This gives the hull a more "modern" look than the other ships. Below the gunwale, there are two parallel strakes made of clay, following the sheer on both sides and joining at the stems. The purpose of these strakes could have been either to strengthen the construction or to protect the hull against injury in touching quays or other boats. To the frames projecting separately above the hull are fastened two horizontal, parallel planks, the lower one outside and the upper one inside the frames, forming a bulwark. In the bow there are catheads for the anchor. Aft, there is a stern gallery, protected by a crescent-shaped pulpit, i.e. a rail supported by stanchions. Across the gunwale between the bulwark and the stern pulpit there is a cross-beam, projecting on both sides of the hull. Inside the hull below the cross-beam there is a small thwart. Sitting with his back against the pulpit is a human figure with arms extended over the cross-beam and resting on the gunwale. The legs or feet of this figure are indicated by dark painted stripes across the thwart. The figure is made in the "snow-man" technique, with a big oval painted eye and eyebrow. Probably the sitting figure ought to represent the helmsman. Aft of the bow stem there is also a short cross-beam or thwart. Inside the hull immediately aft of this bow thwart there is a mast-socket. This item has features similar both to the model in the Kirzis Collection No. 8 and to No. 32 supra.

The model is dated to the Cypro-Archaic period.

51. Clay model of ship.

Fig. 51.

Metropolitan Museum of Art, New York, from the Cesnola Collection, Inv. No. 74.51. 1750.

Provenance: Amathus.

L.P. di Cesnola, *A descriptive Atlas of the Cesnola Collection of Cypriote Antiquities in the Metropolitan Museum of Art in New York, II,* Boston 1885, Pl. LXXVII, No. 701; J.L. Myres, *Handbook of the Cesnola Collection of Antiquities from Cyprus,* New York 1914, 348.

L.o.a. 25.6 cm.

Height amidships 9.2 cm.

Although more roughly made this ship has certain constructional details similar to No. 50 supra – the horizontal strakes along the water-line, the open bulwark or railing, the stern gallery – in this case with two large port-holes for the oars – the prominent catheads at the bow and the helmsman with a steering oar.

The model is of Cypro-Archaic date.

52. Clay model of ship.

Fig. 52.

Metropolitan Museum of Art, New York, from the Cesnola Collection, Inv. No. 74.51.1751.

Provenance: Further provenance in Cyprus unknown.

J.L. Myres, *Handbook of the Cesnola Collection of Antiquities from Cyprus,* New York 1914, 348.

L.o.a. 6 cm.

Height amidships 3 cm.

The clay is rough and uneven. Both the stems project above the gunwale and are slightly curved inwards. The ship has no decoration nor are there any interior fittings except an isolated roughness at the bottom which, however, is not distinct enough to be regarded as a mast-socket.

The model is of Cypro-Archaic date.

53. Oinochoë with a painted ship.

Fig. 53.

British Museum, London, Inv. No. 1926, 6–28.9.

Provenance: Karpas.

Antiquity 32, 1958, 227 Pl. XXIII; Casson, 67, Figs. 95 and 96; Gray, G. 31, 3.c), and 69, Pl. G. I e.f.; V. Karageorghis and J. des Gagniers, *La céramique chypriote de style figuré,* Rome 1974, (Biblioteca di antichità cipriote 2), 122; D.E. McCaslin, *Stone anchors in Antiquity: Coastal settlements and maritime trade-routes in the Eastern Mediterranean ca 1600–1050 B.C.,* Gothenburg 1980, *(SIMA* LXI), 58, Fig. 33 a, with further references.

This jug which belongs to Bichrome IV, is decorated with a black painted ship. Both the stems are highly raised upwards and curved inwards. The aft stem is pointed. The upper part of the fore stem has a comb-like shape. The ship has a mast and stays. The top of the mast is marked by a small round circle. Immediately below this circle, there is a long yard suspended to the mast and running in a curved line between the upper parts of the stems. There is a sail closely bent to this yard. The curve of the yard probably takes its form from the shape of the jug. On each side of the mast there is a large amphora, indicating what type of cargo the ship carried. The lower part of the fore stem is formed like a standing rectangle with five rectangular "windows" or check pattern. This may indicate either a cargo or a fore deck-house.

There are three human figures. One is standing at the stern holding two oars, and must consequently represent the helmsman. One is climbing upon the fore stem, and holding in both hands a rope attached to what must be the anchor, a rounded stone with a round hole in the middle. The third figure is pictured separately outside the ship in a sitting posture. A straight dotted line runs from his buttocks to the mouth of a big fish, probably a shark. The scared expression of this figure, combined with the dotted line, creates the impression of a most dramatic situation.

The jug is dated to the Cypro-Archaic I period, 700–600 BC.

54. Oinochoë with a painted ship.
Fig. 54.
Cyprus Museum, Nicosia, Inv. No. 1947/1–16/1.
Provenance: Further provenance in Cyprus unknown.
Gray, G. 31, 3 b and 72; V. Karageorghis and J. des Gagniers, *La céramique chypriote de style figuré,* Rome 1974, (Biblioteca di antichità cipriote 2) 122–123.

This jug, which belongs to White Painted IV, is decorated with a black painted ship. One of the stems is curved upwards and inwards, with the top formed like a bird's head with the curved beak pointing toward the mast. The other stem rises almost vertically to about the same level as the mast head. The bottom of this stem ends in a small ram, pointing slightly downwards. Amidships there is a mast-socket with a mast. There is a long yard suspended from the mast and running in a curved line between the upper parts of the stems. From the top of the mast two oblique undulating stays run down to the hull. The circle mast head of item 53 is in this case replaced by a triangle pointing downwards. An undulating rope holding an anchor runs from the hull downwards. This rope runs from the same point of the hull where one of the stays is attached. As they represent two separate functions, however, this ought to be a mere coincidence. Across the stem with the bird's head there are two parallel, slightly oblique lines, steering oars, each ending outside the hull in a triangle-shaped part and inside the hull in a grip-handle. Outside the hull, with one foot on the upper triangle-shaped point and one hand on the stem head, there is a human figure. On the other side of the ship outside the hull there is a separate swastika.

The jug is dated to Cypro-Archaic I, 700–600 BC.

55. *Oinochoë with a painted ship.*
Fig. 55.
Metropolitan Museum of Art, New York, from the Cesnola Collection, Inv. No. 74. 51. 511.
Provenance: According to Cesnola found at Ormidia. H. Th. Bossert has not observed that Cesnola has reported about the provenance.
L.P. di Cesnola, *A descriptive Atlas of the Cesnola Collection of Cypriote Antiquities in the Metropolitan Museum of Art in New York II,* Boston 1885, CXXIX, No. 964; J.L. Myres, *Handbook of the Cesnola Collection of Antiquities from Cyprus,* New York 1914, 97; H. Th. Bossert, *Altsyrien,* Tübingen 1951, No. 252. 76; V. Karageorghis and J. des Gagniers, *La céramique chypriote de style figuré,* Rome 1974, (Biblioteca di antichità cipriote 2), 123.

This jug which belongs to White Painted IV, is decorated with a black painted ship. From a roughly crescent-shaped hull the two stems rise upwards. One of them, formed like a bird's head, is pointing inwards. The other stem is pointed and almost vertical. Amidships there is a mast placed on a triangle-shaped mast-socket. Across the top of the mast, between the highest parts of the two stems, there is a yard with a tightly rolled sail. From the point where the yard meets the mast, two oblique stays run down to the gunwale. From the middle of each side of the yard a slightly oblique sheet-line runs down to the foot of the mast-socket. According to Myres, op. cit. 97, there is a fighting deck on open supports in the prow. Another possibility is that this is just a protection for crew or cargo. There are two steering oars, and a kind of gallery indicated by a series of fine rounded arches both in the bow and in the stern.

The jug is of Cypro-Archaic I date.

56. *Graffito of a ship.*
Fig. 56.
Provenance: Salamis, *Cellarka,* Tomb 105.

BCH, 92, 1968, 316–317, Fig. 100; V. Karageorghis, *Salamis in Cyprus*, London 1969, 124; V. Karageorghis, *Excavations in the necropolis of Salamis* II, London 1970, 150 and Pl. CLXXX: 1–4.

On one of the blocks constituting the chamber of tomb No. 105 of the necropolis at Salamis there is a graffito of a ship with a mast supported by a forestay and an aft-stay.

The tomb is dated to c. 600 BC. The blocks, however, are reused. This graffito has a certain similarity to No. 13 supra from Enkomi. Possibly it is as early as No. 13 but lacking further evidence a more exact dating cannot be made.

III HOW THE SHIPS WERE BUILT

HISTORICAL BACKGROUND

From the beginning man must have used whatever material was available to bring him afloat across the waters. When a conscious construction of the first simple raft took place is something we do not know. One of the earliest forms is the skin boat,[1] made of sewn hides around a pre-erected framework. For its production the skin boat required only simple tools and could thus be produced at an early stage of the evolution. Roughly at the same time there existed the clay tub.[2] Both these types of vessels, however – in their first primitive shaping – required sheltered waters free of rocks. Neither type could have withstood the strain of the sea in the same way as a wooden vessel, whether a dug-out or a plank-built boat. Consequently skin boats and clay tubs were found around the Euphrates and the Tigris and in the Nile delta. In this connection it has to be added that a more advanced type of skin boat still exists, the Greenland women's boat, with more seaworthy qualities.

Nor were they unknown in the Greek world to judge, inter alia, from one of the miracles which was performed by Hercules when voyaging in a pot. Skin boats and clay tubs still exist in various parts of the world.

No. 25 in the catalogue, dated to Cypro-Archaic times, has certain hull features which indicate the possibility, however slight, that it could have been a skin boat. The simple explanation, on the other hand, may be that these features are only the finger-marks of the maker. It is probable that skin boats appeared in Cyprus only as an exception considering the vast resources of timber, the natural geographical conditions and the relevant demand for seaworthiness. The next step in the evolution is represented by the bark canoe and the dug-out. The bark canoe can be made without tools, and the dug-out requires only a few simple tools together with a controlled use of fire. Chronologically and geographically, the dug-out can be traced from the Stone Age to the fifth century A.D. and from Spain to India.[3]

Cyprus was well forested before the Hellenistic period and logically the supply of timber offered good opportunities for production of dug-outs and bark canoes. The outstanding qualities of wood are its strength and elasticity, its lightness and the ease with which it can be handled. The choice of wood was, of course, due to local conditions. In Cyprus according to Theophrastus, local pine was preferred to fir, as it seemed to be better suited for boat construction.[4]

All these types of boats, rafts, clay tubs, skin boats, bark canoes and dug-outs can be made with very simple tools and consequently at an early stage by comparatively primitive people. Except the dug-out and perhaps, as has been mentioned above, the skin boat, they all have their limitations and are difficult to develop. The limitations of the skin boat and the clay tubs have already been mentioned, and the size and strength of the bark canoe are entirely dependent on the bark. The dug-out, on the other hand, had all possibilities of development and had the main influence on the subsequent construction of boats.

Many of the items in the catalogue are canoe-shaped as Nos. 11, 17, 24, 29, 34 and 36. Of course ships of later date could have been built of bark, but probably the bark canoe shape was preserved by tradition, even if the material and the way of building had changed.

When man started to make rafts is unclear. The first known attempts to reshape the reed rafts into what could be called a vessel with bow and stern were made in Egypt during the second half of the fourth millennium BC.[5] The shape and rigging of these craft influenced the construction of their first wooden vessels. Roughly from the same time there is the oldest known clay model of a boat, found in a tomb at Eridu in Mesopotamia,[6] dated to around 3400 BC.

Certain items in the catalogue are rather similar to the Eridu boat, even if not from the same time and even if there is not full correspondence in all details. The interior of No. 33 recalls the Eridu boat, and No. 19 has a mast-socket and holes in the hull placed in about the same way. The supposition that the Eridu boat has a mast-socket and that the holes in the gunwale were fastening points for stays and shrouds is, of course, as Casson remarks, not sure.[7] However, I do not think that his alternative suggestion that the purpose of the socket would be to hold some ceremonial staff is more plausible. I am more inclined to think that they are a mast-socket and holes for stays, as the socket is very similar to the sockets of Nos. 19, 31, 33, 48, 50 and 51.

The art of shipbuilding has always been bound by tradition, and probably sails existed already during the fourth millennium BC, even if this has been impossible to prove up to now.

The fourth millennium BC also gives us the first written sources. Among many pictograms on clay tablets there is a representation of a boat with high stems not unlike the graffiti of ships from the temple wall of Kition, No. 14.

The embryo of shipbuilding in a modern sense – keel, stems, ribs and strakes – grew out of the dug-out, and started in Egypt about 3000 BC. It was developed by the Aegeans especially during the so-called Minoan thalassocracy, when new creations and main inventions were born.[8] To judge by an Egyptian relief from about 1500 BC there existed wooden ships well over 200 feet long.[9] Gradually the long and slender type of craft was replaced by a rounded type of hull, both for rowing galleys and sailing vessels.

CONSTRUCTION METHOD

Two methods of construction of a wooden boat can be distinguished.[10] With the shell construction, introduced by the Egyptians, the hull was first built up plank by plank and the ribs subsequently inserted for reinforcement. With the skeleton construction the keel, stems and ribs were first raised, after which the planking was added. Certain construction details changed, but building the shell way was predominant in the whole Mediterranean in ancient times. One does not know when skeleton construction was more widely accepted. It may, however, have been well into the Middle Ages.

The first step taken by the Mediterranean ship-builder was to lay down first the keel and then the strakes which he joined edge to edge in a bricklaying fashion, and then held together by mortise and tenon, further fastening them with fibre ropes. Afterwards, the hull was strengthened with wooden cross-beams and caulked from the inside with fibre. The frames were always inserted later. These did not have to be very strong, and their number was often due to the economy of the boat-builder. The application of the frames could even wait until the boat had been in use for a long time and the hull had started to weaken.

Certain construction details gradually changed but shipbuilding BC was comparatively conservative and no radical changes seem to have taken place in the Mediterranean from the Bronze to the Byzantine Age. The knowledge and the information we have of how the boats were built is mainly based on ships from Egypt and on wrecks from later dates. Of special interest of course, is the Kyrenia wreck, which in every respect confirms the details given above.[11]

The limited scale of this very coarse and primitive material has been emphasized, and thus I can only note that the material available does not give any clue to the question whether the shell or the skeleton way of building was used. On the other hand there is no reason to assume anything else than that the Cypriote boats also followed the traditional pattern, with shell construction with reinforcements inside and outside the hull. The Kazaphani boat, No. 5, has marked reinforcements on the inside, fastened with bolts, and also on the outside. Nos. 38 and 50 have reinforcements on the outside of the hull. Nos. 19 and 26 have, inside the hull, painted lines drawn from gunwale to gunwale which must be considered to represent frames but which, unfortunately, cannot contribute to a definite opinion whether the boat was built by the shell or the skeleton method.

CERTAIN SHIPBUILDING DETAILS

Keel

Cyprus was well forested before the Hellenistic period and there was plenty of suitable material for shipbuilding. There was also the possibility of getting longer planks than, for example, in Egypt, and thus the hull could be raised from the keel plank in a more efficient and continuous way. No. 5 has a clearly marked keel plank inside the hull, widening towards the stems.

Ship No. 32 has a painted black line running inside the hull from stem to stem and is the only one in the catalogue which has a kelson marked in this way. Nos. 23 and 50, on the other hand, have clearly marked clay keels. The painted line on No. 17 could also possibly be interpreted as a keel.

Also No. 19 has a line on the outside of the hull which can be interpreted as a keel strake. The limitations of the material in number as well as quality make me hesitant to draw any conclusions from these observations. However, the material indicates that the boats during the Bronze Age seem to have had no keel, and this seems to have been the case also in Geometric times. It is first during the Cypro-Archaic period that keel in the modern sense seems to begin to appear, although it may have been found already during Cypro-Geometric III. A similar conclusion has been drawn by J.S. Morrison via keel-less ships built in Egypt from the third millennium and the Cape Gelidonya ship, which probably had no keel to the Kyrenia ship which had a keel.[12]

Thwarts

Part of the construction of the hull are also the thwarts, which could have served both as a reinforcement to hold together the hull and as benches for the crew. Thwarts appear on many of the models, Nos. 7, 8, 20, 23, 24, 32, 33, 37, 42, 43 and 50. The most common form is two thwarts, one in the bow and one in the stern, as on Nos. 7, 20, 24, 31, 33 and 50. These thwarts are so modelled that they rest upon the gunwale and protrude outside the hull. Nos. 23 and 32 have four thwarts. Those in the bow and the stern rest upon the gunwale and the two middle ones are fastened to the inside of the hull. Nos. 8, 37, 42 and 43 have each one thwart. Concerning Nos. 42 and 43, however, it has to be remarked that they are both incomplete and only parts of clay models. No. 8 as well as No. 7 have a thwart resting upon the gunwale and protruding outside the hull.

It is not improbable that the bow and stern thwarts resting upon the gunwale may have had the double function both to serve as a seat for the crew and to be part of the construction to keep the hull toghether.

Ram

In this connection, the very controversial question of the ram ought to be discussed, as the ram, in my opinion, was originally a purely constructional detail and any special functions were later inventions.

A ram appears on a great number of the boats in the catalogue, Nos. 19, 20, 24, 30, 37, 39, 40, 41, 42 and 46, all belonging to the Cypro-Archaic period. On all the Cypriote models, the ram appears at the bow as a prolongation forward of the keel or the bottom line. Here it has to be remarked that No. 17 also has a cutwater.

The Cypriote material with ram consists of both so-called round and long boats. As a rule round boats are considered to be merchant ships and long boats men-of-war. I will revert to this question later on. Rams appeared already on very early representations, for example on a clay box from Pylos and a vase from Asine, 1200–1100 BC.[13] From being a harmless and peaceful prolongation of the stem on Bronze Age ships the ram developed into an offensive weapon in naval encounters, which were radically changed through this new technique. Earlier the man-of-war crews had fought each other in the same way as in battles ashore, but now the ship itself became an offensive weapon through the ram. This type of naval warfare reached its peak during the age of the triremes, 500–323 BC.[14]

One of the reasons for the different points of view on the ram has been the question which is stern and bow, as many models, both on seals and in clay show a high stem with a distinctive projection at the water-line. In connection with the discovery of the Thera wall-paintings, Casson remarks temperamentally that it closes the long debate about the shape of the Bronze Age craft. "When in a Bronze Age representation of a ship a pronounced waterline projection appears, this is the stern."[15] The question does not concern only the Bronze Age boats, but boats right up to the time of the trireme. Casson's opinion is not shared by Morrison.[16] I am most inclined to agree with Morrison. Above all, I am attracted by his purely practical idea that the helmsman must have a clear view forwards, and that consequently the lower stem is the bow. The same practical reasoning lies behind his conclusion "And the up-curving stern facilitates the manoeuvre of beaching, which in Homer is always carried out stern first."[17]

The wall-paintings from Thera are, of course, very confusing. Casson suggests that the purpose of the stern ram would be to have a stabilizing effect on the boat.[18] Marinatos as well as Morrison suggest as an explanation that the stern projection of the Thera ships is an embarcation step and a lavatory platform.[19]

In the Cypriote material there are no Bronze Age boats with rams. The first indication is the cutwater of No. 17. In all other cases from Cypro-Archaic times the ram appears at the bow as a prolongation of the bottom board or the keel, a construction which later developed into the warship ram. Whether any man-of-war with a ram appears in the Cypriote material is a question I shall revert to in the chapter "Types of ships".

The discussion regarding what is bow and what is stern as well as regarding the function of the ram continues, quite recently in an article by P.F. Johnston.[20]

The discovery of the Thera wall-paintings has widened our knowledge of Bronze Age ships and raises new questions which, however, have not yet been answered in a satisfactory way.

The very central question of what is bow and what is stern is unfortunately not solved in an unequivocal way by this. A great number of the items are symmetrical and the Cypriote material only gives some clue to a solution when the presence of a helmsman contributes to indicate the stern.

Deck

When the hull had been completed and the frames inserted, the next question to be solved was how to construct a deck able to function both as a shelter for the cargo and the crew and as a platform for the helmsman and passengers. With a deck, of course, the ships also became more seaworthy.

On Nos. 1 and 23 there is a shelter or half deck. On No. 1 it is very small and it is difficult to draw any conclusion regarding its function. The half deck of No. 23 is more clearly marked and evidently serves both as a place for the helmsman and a protected space for the cargo. Poop-decks also appear to a limited extent in the material, viz. on Nos. 8, 32 and 50 as a conspicuous and advanced construction. The poop-deck of No. 50 is unusual, as it is placed outside the stern with projections outside the hull, probably to gain more space. Nos. 11 and 35 have also minor traces of what could be a poop-deck.

Tumble-home and scuppers

Three of the items in the catalogue, Nos. 8, 32 and 41 have a pronounced tumble-home, which must be considered to be a fairly advanced technique in shipbuilding. The reason for this construction could be a lowering of the centre of gravity to acquire a steadying effect, to get a larger and more sheltered space for the cargo and to create a flatter hull to enable the ship to enter more shallow waters.

The tumble-home is an interesting detail in shipbuilding and shows, among other things, that the Cypriotes were not ignorant of rather advanced ideas. The tumble-home as a construction detail has existed up to modern times, even if it now seems to have been abandoned by our modern yacht designers.

The question of the hull also includes such a detail as scuppers. Nos. 8 and 32, which are among the technically most advanced models in the catalogue, have among other things holes through the hull which could be interpreted as scuppers. The primary purpose of the scuppers is to facilitate the drainage of water from a deck. Not one of these models, however, has a deck or even a trace of an ordinary deck, nor are they damaged or incomplete. On the other hand, it cannot be excluded that ships of this size with so many technical details could have had such arrangements, and that the maker has had this in mind. Otherwise these holes could, of course, be interpreted as holes for oars, fastening points for stays or holes to secure the cargo.

TO SUM UP

To conclude this part I should like to emphasize that the material available does not show for certain if the shell or the skeleton method was used in the construction of the hull. However, I do not find any reason not to assume that on Cyprus the same method of boat-building was used as in other parts of the eastern Mediterranean, i.e. the shell method with subsequent reinforcements. As a rule the boats have been equipped with two thwarts, small decks in the bow and the stern, but otherwise open. In my opinion the bow projection, as I have remarked above, was originally a purely constructional detail in connection with the laying of the keel until the time of the triremes when the ram was given a new function as an offensive weapon.

At any rate both tumble-home and perhaps also scuppers indicate that the Cypriotes were able and experienced shipbuilders.

NOTES: CHAPTER III

1. Casson, 5–6.
2. Casson, 7.
3. Casson, 8.
4. Casson, 212, note 51.
5. Casson, 11–12.
6. Casson, Fig. 20.
7. Casson, 22.
8. Casson, 30, 38–39.
9. Casson, 17.
10. Casson, 201–216; B. Greenhill, *Archaeology of the boat*, London 1976, 64, 72.
11. *National Geographic Magazine,* January 1954, 1–36, June 1970, 841–857; M.L. Katzev, 'The Kyrenia ship' in G.F. Bass, *A history of seafaring based on underwater archaeology*, London 1972, 50–52.
12. J.S. Morrison, 'The Classical traditions' in B. Greenhill, *Archaeology of the boat*, London 1976, 160–162.
13. Casson, Figs. 28 and 29.
14. Casson, 80–81; G.F. Bass, *A history of seafaring based on underwater archaeology*, London 1972, 22; J.S. Morrison, 'The Classical traditions', in B. Greenhill, *Archaeology of the boat*, London 1976, 157.
15. L. Casson, 'Bronze Age ships. The evidence of the Thera wall paintings', *The International Journal of Nautical Archaeology 4*, London 1975, 9.
16. J.S. Morrison, 'The Classical traditions' in B. Greenhill, *Archaeology of the boat*, London 1976, 156–157.
17. J.S. Morrison (supra note 16), 157.
18. Casson (supra note 15), 8–9.
19. J.S. Morrison (supra note 16), 156; S. Marinatos, 'Das Schiffsfresko von Akrotiri, Thera' in D. Gray, *Seewesen,* Göttingen 1974 (= *Archaeologia Homerica* Band I, Kap. G) G. 147–148.
20. P.F. Johnston, 'Bronze Age Cycladic Ships', in *Temple University Aegean Symposium* 7, 1982, 1–6.

IV MOTIVE POWER – ROWING OR SAILING

From the beginning the boats were propelled by paddles which were later consistently replaced – around 2400 BC – by oars on larger vessels. The oars were short, with the result that the oarsmen had to stand up to be able to dip the oar blades in the water.[1]

We do not know when man began to use the wind as a motive power, but the oldest unmistakable pictures of sailing craft are of Egyptian origin.[2]

In the catalogue material evidence can be found that Cypriote boats also were driven by oars or sails and sometimes by both.

There are representations of sails on only three ships, No. 13, a graffito from Enkomi with a swelling sail in a fair wind, and Nos. 53 and 55, where the sail is tightly rolled to a yard. There is only one sail, square or rectangular, and no head-sail, which implies that the boats could only be sailed in a following wind but were not able to sail to windward. Graffito No. 13 does not indicate if the sail was equipped with a boom along the foot. The Thera wall-paintings show that the sails were sometimes equipped with a boom, a detail of sail construction which had been suggested earlier by Casson.[3] The Cypriote material is too rudimentary to allow any conclusions in this matter.

Even if there are no more representations of sails there are many examples of masts, mast-sockets and stays, indicating that the ships had been equipped with sails.

Three models of L.C. date, Nos. 5, 6 and 8 have a mast-socket amidships as well as Nos. 19, 23, 26, 31, 32, 33, 48, 50, 51, 54 and 55 from Cypro-Archaic times.

No. 5 has not only a mast-socket but also a row of holes along the gunwale, which could have been used for fastening stays, sheet-lines or lines for securing the cargo. As far as Nos. 6, 8, 19 and 32 are concerned the same reflections present themselves regarding the purpose of the row of holes as on No. 5. Neither can it be excluded that the row of holes of Nos. 5, 6, 8 and 32 were also used for rowing.

Probably these boats have been equipped both with oars and sails. Most ships on the temple wall at Kition, No. 14, have a mast. The same applies to the graffiti of the altar at Kition, No. 15, as well as to the graffiti from Enkomi, No. 13 and from Salamis No. 56. The representation of a ship on a cylinder, No. 16, shows a mast. The ship paintings on the vases of the catalogue, Nos. 18, 53, 54 and 55 all have masts. The mast of No. 23 has not only a socket but also a crow's nest on the top, in which a figure is placed who must be considered to be the look-out man.

A common feature in the material is that the masts as well as the mast-sockets are placed amidships.

Usually mast and sail were taken down and placed on the deck or in the boat when not in use.[4] The Cypriote material, however, does not give us any information in this matter.

The mast was kept in place by fore and aft stays.[5] In antiquity standing rigging is often depicted with one forestay and one aft-stay. This rigging appears on Nos. 16, 18, 54, 55 and 56. According to Homer there sometimes existed two forestays which is not the case in the Cypriote material.

The running rig consists of halyards, sheets and all moving ropes connected with the sail. The function of the halyards is to hoist the sail, the function of the sheets to handle it when hoisted. Even if the representation is primitive and the material scanty, a running rigging may be traced on items Nos. 18, 53, 54 and 55. The primitive conception of the problems of perspective also makes it difficult to form an opinion of what the various lines represent. The clearest example of standing and running rigging is No. 55, where the lines from the top of the mast can be interpreted as stays and the lines from the yard as halyards or sheets.

The first boats were propelled by paddling or rowing, and even when sails came into use a combination with oars could offer an even speed and a reliable performance. Considering wind conditions in the Mediterranean and the fact that sailing could only be mastered in a following wind the auxiliary power of the oars was often essential.[6]

The act of rowing is only represented by the material on No. 12 and I have interpreted the human figure with an oar, No. 21, as the helmsman.

In the literature of marine archaeology, oblique lines outside the hull and holes along the gunwale are as a rule interpreted as the wish of the maker or the artist to describe oars.

Evidently one has to be careful not to draw any conclusions regarding the size of the boat guided by the number of lines and holes. As far as painted oblique lines are concerned, these may have been due only to the desire of the artist to fill an empty space with a decoration and, as I have already pointed out, holes could also have other functions as fastening points.

In antiquity, during the period covered by this study, boats were rowed from the gunwale or from a lower deck.[8] I consider the painted oblique lines on the outside of the hulls of Nos. 16, 19, 20, 27 and 39 as undoubtedly representing oars. On the other hand, I consider the lines of No. 37 too obscure to give any clue regarding their function. Also the lines of No. 30, two fore and two aft, are difficult to interpret. They could possibly be a mere decoration. The row of holes along the gunwale of some of the items, Nos. 5, 6, 7, 8, 11, 19 and 32, I regard as possible oar holes.

The holes along the gunwale of Nos. 1 and 3, on the other hand, give the impression of having served as fastening points for a suspension device.

Concerning Nos. 8 and 32, some of the holes could have been for the oars and possibly some, the larger ones, could be interpreted as scuppers.

It has to be remarked that the holes of Nos. 11 and 32 are placed somewhat below the gunwale, which is marked on both items by a painted line. One hypothesis could be that the maker wanted to describe the boat as being rowed both from the gunwale, and from a lower deck. This arrangement appears inter alia in reproductions of warships from about 750–550 BC.[9]

On the whole, it is not possible categorically to regard these rows of holes as oar holes. As I have mentioned above they may also have served other purposes.

In antiquity, the boat was generally steered by two oversized oars, one on the starboard side and one on the port side.[10] The steering oars were fastened to the side of the boat in various ways. On large sailing vessels they were exposed to a heavy strain, and were often sheltered by wing-like projections on the quarters. The boat was steered almost always by one man.

On smaller craft, there also appeared a steering oar on the starboard quarter. Casson mentions No. 23 as an example but he must have been mistaken.[11] There are, in fact, the remains of a steering oar on the port side. No. 21, however, can serve as an example. The helmsman is sitting in the stern holding a steering oar in his hand. A helmsman with two oars appears on Nos. 23, 51, 53, 54 and 55. No. 16, which is a seal, shows a helmsman with one steering oar, probably owing to the maker's inability to illustrate two steering oars. On No. 55 two steering oars have been painted, and Nos. 8 and 50 have holes for steering oars. No. 32 has shafts for steering oars. According to the excavation report an iron oar was also found, but this, is now lost, however. The steering oars of No. 32 are housed in a tower-like projection which has no earlier ancient parallel.[12] No. 50, a clay model, has a figure sitting in the stern on a poop-deck or outrigger. He must be considered to be the helmsman. Some of the lines on No. 39 could possibly be interpreted as steering oars, viz. the ones painted separately from the other oblique lines. At last, the graffito No. 56 has two steering oars.

TO SUM UP

From the available material it seems evident hat most of the ships have been equipped with sails and that the combination of sails and oars has been usual among the Cypriote ships. It also appears that the steering was performed by the boats being manoeuvred by two steering oars and that even small craft were steered with an oar. As is still done today small boats were also, of course, often manoeuvred with the rowing oars only.

NOTES: CHAPTER IV

1. Casson, 18.
2. Casson, 12, Fig. 6.
3. S. Marinatos, 'Das Schiffsfresko von Akrotiri, Thera' in D. Gray, *Seewesen,* Göttingen 1974 (= *Archaeologia Homerica,* Band I, Kap. G) G. 149; Casson, 33; L. Casson, 'Bronze Age ships. The evidence of the Thera wall paintings', *The International Journal of Nautical Archaeology,* 4, London 1975, 6.
4. Casson, 19, 47.
5. Casson, 47, 69.
6. Casson, 65.
7. Casson, 54.
8. Casson, 55.
9. Casson, Figs. 72, 76, 78 and 83.
10. Casson, 224; M.-Ch. de Graeve, *The ships of the ancient Near East (c. 2000–500 B.C.),* Leuven 1981, 172–173.
11. Casson, 329.
12. Casson, 66, note 113.

V DECORATION

As the size of most of the items in the catalogue material is so small, it is almost surprising that there has been space for other decoration than simple lines in various colours, and that such particular details appear as eyes, animal's heads and fish-tails. In other words the same decoration as can still be seen today on Mediterranean boats.

Merely eyes without a connection with an animal's head, appear on Nos. 30 and 39 and, according to the excavation report, also on No. 32, where, however, this decoration has now disappeared. All the eyes are painted and appear on models from Cypro-Archaic times. In our world of imagination, a representation of an eye has been supposed to help the seafarer to keep a right course and to avoid danger, i.e. an apotropaic function, but according to Gray there is nothing to support the idea that an eye should have had either an entirely decorational or a magical function.[1]

Considering the eye and the ram it has been suggested that the Greeks shaped the whole ram like a boar's head.[2] This should have taken place roughly about 600 BC. In the Cypriote material there appear three unmistakable examples, Nos. 24, 40 and 41, which must be considered to represent boar's heads with eyes and ram. Concerning No. 20, when studying the original I have in the first place got the impression that the bow head has had a certain resemblance to a dolphin. On the photographs, however, it has many similarities to the other boars' heads.

On Nos. 10, 21, 54 and 55 there are bird-like animals. On No. 21 I consider that the bird is placed in the bow, and that there is a helmsman in the stern, steering the boat. On Nos. 54 and 55, on the other hand, I consider the bird's heads to be placed in the stern, facing forwards, which also appears on Greek vases.[3] On Nos. 21 and 54 the birds have eyes. According to Casson "the goose-head is said to be the decoration par excellence of merchantmen".[4] The bow of No. 17 has been interpreted as a representation of a bird's head.[5] Even if I do not consider the similarity sufficiently evident, it could, of course, represent a goose-head.

No. 1, dating from the Middle Cypriote I period, has two small bird-like objects sitting on the gunwale among eight human figures. What the boat, its crew and the birds represent is something we can only guess. Possibly, as Åström suggests, it is a married couple on its way to the kingdom of death or the celebration of a so-called sacred marriage.[6]

Eyes appear in the Cypriote material both on birds and boars, as well as single eyes, even if they are perhaps not as frequent as Gray suggests.[7]

Fish-tails appear on Nos. 10, 33, 42, 43 and 45. The fish-tails, which can sometimes be not very clearly shaped by the maker, are described in the literature as forked, rowlock-like or as a bifurcation of the stem. This concerns a relatively small number, and a definite solution of the matter requires more evidence.[8] Even if only Cretan material has been discussed in this connection, I see no reason not to assume that it is also applicable to the Cypriote material. I do not know if much more can be got from it than that a maritime shape is a good and logical finishing off of the stem.

Other decoration is connected with the nature, shape and technical features of the material, and is of importance for the dating, for example Nos. 2 and 3 which are White Painted IV Ware.

TO SUM UP

The decoration appearing in the Cypriote material is infrequent, but must nevertheless be considered to correspond with and to follow the decoration on other boats in the eastern Mediterranean area.

NOTES: CHAPTER V

1. Gray, G. 60.
2. G.F. Bass, *A history of seafaring based on underwater archaeology*, London 1972, 42; Gray, G. 63–65; Casson, 64.
3. Casson, 38.
4. Casson, 347–348.
5. M.-Ch. de Graeve, *The ships of the Ancient near East (c. 2000–500 B.C.)*, Leuven 1981, 124.
6. P. Åström, 'Cypern – en kulturhistorisk och konsthistorisk skiss' in *Cypern – motsättningarnas ö*, Gothenburg 1974, (*SIMA* Pocket-book 1), 19.
7. Gray, G. 69.
8. Casson, 33.

VI CREW

Among the ships in the catalogue Nos. 1, 2, 3, 12, 16, 21, 22, 23, 26, 27, 28, 44, 49, 50, 51, 53 and 54 are manned.

The position and postures of these human figures seem to indicate some sailors' activity such as look-out on No. 23 and helmsman on Nos. 16, 21, 23, 50, 51, 53 and 54. The two figures of No. 12 are very schematic but seem to have oars in their hands for rowing. The second figure of No. 53, who is not a helmsman, seems to be a sailor dropping a heavy anchor into the sea by means of some kind of boom. The remaining human figures do not seem to be engaged in any particular activity to do with the ship and the sea. Many of the figures are placed in a resting position with their arms on the gunwale, as Nos. 3, 22, 26, 27, 28, 44 and 49.

As far as the figures on board ship No. 1 are concerned, sitting around the gunwale, some with their hands on the gunwale, others embracing each other, the impression is primarily that the ship may have had a religious or ceremonial purpose as mentioned above under the chapter "Decoration". This impression is emphasized by the bird-like objects also placed on the gunwale. Some of the figures have no indication of their sex, while the figures of No. 21, the helmsman, and Nos. 22, 23, 26, 44 and 50 seem to be men made in the "snow-man" technique.

On board No. 26 there is an animal, probably a sheep or a dog. The shape and the equipment of this ship give the impression of a small craft. Probably the ship could have been used for transport of domestic animals in the same way as today with caiques between the islands. It could also have been only for household fishing, the owner having brought his dog. Since the provenance of this item is unknown, a third alternative might be that it concerns a grave find with a sacrificial animal.

TO SUM UP

The human figures do not give many clues to the problem of whether the ships were operated by rowing or sailing, only that helmsmen and look-outs have existed and some kind of rowing action is represented on No. 12.

Whatever these functions may involve, painted oblique lines, on the other hand, as on Nos. 16, 19 and 20, and rows of holes in the gunwale as on Nos. 5, 6, 7 and 8 give a clear indication that the boats were propelled by rowers, as has been discussed in chapter IV. Even if one has to be careful in estimating the number of rowers, and to take into consideration the space required by each rower when drawing any conclusions as to the size of the boat, Nos. 5, 6, 7, 11 and 19 particularly, indicate a number of up to c. 40 rowers on each side. According to estimations a rower requires about 3 feet.[1] Concerning Nos. 11 and 32 I have furthermore wondered if there could have been two rows of rowers, i.e. one rowing from the gunwale and one from a lower deck. Possibly there could have been up to 25 or 30 rowers on each side.[2]

This indicates that certain of the boats of the catalogue have had a considerable size and consequently needed a large crew. Moreover there appear in the catalogue material many small undecked boats, for example Nos. 22, 37, 49 and 52, which were presumably propelled by rowers in the same way as is still done today.

NOTES: CHAPTER VI

1. Casson, 22.
2. Casson, 58–59.

VII ANCHORS AND OTHER EQUIPMENT

Anchors appear on Nos. 53 and 54, in both cases so-called weight anchors.[1] This type of anchor was stopped by stones and reefs on the sea bottom and functioned through its mere weight, which was often more than 100 kilos. Usually in antiquity boats brought different types of anchors to be prepared for all eventualities.[2] Other types, as for example the composite anchor with other qualifications than the weight anchor, were also used on Cyprus but are not documented by the material of this catalogue. On No. 53 it seems as if a member of the crew is using a boom to cast the heavy anchor.[3]

Some of the boats, viz. Nos. 8, 32, 38, 50 and 51, have catheads from which the anchor-line ran, and where it could also be fastened. No. 8 has four catheads, two fore and two aft. No. 38 is only a part of a boat and has only two. Nos. 32 and 50 have each two distinct catheads but it is possible that certain protruding pieces can be interpreted as additional catheads. This would mean that also these models had four catheads each. As remarked above, it was usual that boats in antiquity brought many types of anchors, and it is very possible that anchors were cast both from the bow and from the stern.

It was also usual for boats to have cork on board, as well as tools for the carpenter.[4] The cork was used either as marking buoys for the anchors or as a life-saving device. The Cypriote material does not give us any information in this matter. Considering the primitive character of the material, this would perhaps be asking too much.

Belaying pins appear on Nos. 5 and 26. There are two on No. 5, one on each side of the mast-socket. They were probably used for fastening the halyards. On No. 26 there are two fragments which can be interpreted as belaying pins and which give rise to the same reflection.

NOTES: CHAPTER VII

1. H. Frost, 'From rope to chain on the development of anchors in the Mediterranean', *The Mariner's Mirror* 49, 1963, 7–10, Fig. 1.; D.E. McCaslin, *Stone anchors in Antiquity: Coastal settlements and maritime trade-routes in the Eastern Mediterranean ca. 1600–1050 B.C.,* Gothenburg 1980, (*SIMA* LXI), 18, Fig. 6, 23, Fig. 10, 1, II.
2. D.E. McCaslin (supra note 1), 20; Casson, 255.
3. D.E. McCaslin (supra note 1), 58.
4. Casson, 257.

VIII TYPES OF SHIPS

It is difficult to judge and to interpret the material covered by this study as there are no known real Cypriote ships or wrecks for comparison, and I have had to depend entirely on representations of ships as sources. The only wreck found in the Mediterranean which coincides with my material is from Cape Gelidonya and is dated to about 1200 BC. Unfortunately its condition is such that it gives little information regarding construction etc. The finds from the wreck outside Kyrenia on Cyprus dated to the late fourth century BC give more information, but do not quite coincide with my material. The Kyrenia wreck, however, can be regarded as a confirmation that the shell method of construction was used and the strakes joined together by mortise and tenon. Most of the items in this study are dated to the period between these two wrecks. It has to be kept in mind that the clay models as well as the other representations are made without yardstick, and that their size and other dimensions convey to us only a fragmentary reflection of the reality behind. Thus there exists very little parallel material available, and most ships in the catalogue are very crudely made.

Some ships are long and slender, some are shorter and more tubby, and there has been a tendency to classify the long ones as men-of-war and the round ones as merchant vessels. Even if later on this classification could be correct in general it does not always agree with the way the ships were used. The long, slender ships may also have functioned as transport and merchant vessels, and pure men-of-war have not yet been documented before probably the first half of the 7th century, even that dating being uncertain.[1] In naval warfare in ancient times, the ships were mostly used as means of transport for the warriors, but the actual fighting took place ashore.

Actually, it seems that it was in the time of the trireme that the ship began to function in actual warfare with the ram as an offensive weapon. The projecting parts which later on developed into the ram were, in my view, only a constructional detail, an extension of the keel or the kelson, and had nothing to do with the classification of the ships during the period covered by this study. Nor did Homer mention the ram in his rather detailed account of how Odysseus built his boat. However, one must take it for granted that the round and roomy ships were merchantmen, with their special need of space for cargo and crew.

Often the round ships are symmetrical, i.e. both ends are equally high, while the long ships have a high stern and a lower fore part. Nor is it certain, or a rule, that the symmetrical ships were always cargo vessels and the unsymmetrical ones men-of-war. An Assyrian relief from c. 700 BC for example shows men-of-war which are both symmetrical and unsymmetrical, possibly representing both ships taking active part in the fighting and ships used for soldier transport.[2]

In his criticism of Gray's book "Seewesen", S.C. Humphreys says, among other things, that her classification of representations of Bronze Age ships into two distinct categories, "galleys" and "caiques", seems to him dubious[3]. I feel inclined to agree with Humphreys, and I am furthermore hesitant about this category grouping also for later periods. During the actual period covered by this study it seems most unlikely that special men-of-war existed. Only one of the Cypriote ships, No. 46, has been classified in the literature as a man-of-war. This model has not a specially pronounced ram, and the dating is uncertain. Nor has it any arrangements for sailing or rowing. Furthermore, the model is primitively and crudely made. I am not convinced that it is a representation of a man-of-war. The ram is not in itself a sufficient argument and I refer in this matter to my previous presumption that the ram is a technical prolongation of the keel. The aim of the maker could, of course, have been to represent a merchant vessel, but I would rather place this item in that rather diffuse category of ships regarding the function of which no definite conclusion can be drawn.

Consequently, it is my opinion that the Cypriote material mainly represents ships for peaceful purposes.

The catalogue includes representations of a great variety of ships, probably ranging from large merchant vessels to small boats for household fishing. Models of boats for coastal trade appear, as well as larger craft for trade.

Roughly the material can be divided into three groups. I except Nos. 1 and 2 as having a religious connection and the graffiti representations Nos. 14 and 15 as being very schematical, and not yet fully published by their excavator.

GROUP 1

To this group I should like to assign some items which, irrespective of their size, have such features and technical details that they must be regarded as representations of large sailing vessels for carrying cargo on the high seas. These ships also demonstrate the knowledge and technical skill of the Cypriotes in the art of shipbuilding. The items in this first category are Nos. 5, 6, 7, 8, 32, 50, 51, 53, 54 and 55, with special emphasis on Nos. 8, 32 and 50 which have poop-deck and robust arrangements for steering oars. To that can be added such a sophisticated feature as tumble-home on Nos. 8 and 32. Furthermore, all of these items have arrangements both for sailing and rowing.

The Homeric boat for ordinary dispatch had 20 oars.[4] A penteconter had 50. This was a boat with 25 oarsmen on each side, probably about 30 m. long and with a mast of at least 10 m.[5] A text from Ugarit from c. 1200 BC mentions a cargo of 450 tons as something not unusual.[6] Item No. 5 from Kazaphani has, in all, 75 holes in the gunwale, and even if some of the holes were fastening points for stays and sheets, or for ropes to secure the cargo, the intention seems to have been to show that the ship was propelled by a great number of oarsmen and was consequently of a considerable size.

The same reflection applies to the Maroni ships Nos. 6 and 7, both of which have 18 holes in the gunwale on each side. If my interpretation is correct, that Nos. 8 and 32 both have two rows of oarsmen on each side, one at the gunwale level and one further below, it could perhaps indicate 60 oarsmen on each side. This would consequently mean that there are representations of ships of considerable size, sea-going vessels able to cross the seas by means of sails and oars.

GROUP 2

To group number 2 I should like to assign what I regard as the prototype for the ancient Cypriote boats, a prototype which has many features similar to those of the caique of today in the eastern Mediterranean area. The hulls are broad and deep with good space for cargo and crew. They were propelled by means of sails or oars or sometimes by both, depending on weather and wind. According to Homer, the ordinary boat had 20 oars, as mentioned above, and many of the boats in this group seem to fit into this size. The boats are undecked, possibly sometimes with a smaller deck fore and aft. This group covers the majority of the items in the catalogue, for example Nos. 9, 10, 16, 19, 20, 23, 25, 31, 33, 34, 40, 41, 45, 48 and 56. These boats may have been used for transport of passengers and goods. In spite of all reservations for horror vacui or artist's exaggeration when decorating the ship, lack of yardstick etc., it seems that this type of boat is smaller than those I have considered suitable for inclusion in group 1. At the same time it must be emphasized that a boat need not necessarily be very large to be able to cross open waters.

Some of the boats placed in group 2 have a low freeboard for example Nos. 11, 17, 24, 26 and 34, and can be regarded principally as coasters. Furthermore, they have no arrangements for sailing.

GROUP 3

To the third group belong among others Nos. 12, 22, 27, 30, 37 and 52, which in the main can be classified as small boats. Their type and appearance vary, probably in accordance with ideas and traditions of the local boatbuilders. None of them has sails, mast or other equipment for sailing, which indicates that they must have been propelled by rowing. No. 12 is the only item in the catalogue showing oarsmen. Some of the boats, however, are manned, but the figures are placed in a resting position and do not seem to be engaged in any type of sailor's activity.

There is also in the material a diffuse group of boats which, with a slight hesitation can be placed in both group 2 and group 3. There are finally some fragments of clay models which give no clue to the purpose of the boat which they represent, and consequently to the category in which it should be classified. In all, the distinctions between the various types sometimes seem rather vague.

The lack of real ships for comparison has justified me in including in this study Homer's account of Odysseus' boat and how it was built. The text of the Odyssey also presents many interesting details which together give a rather clear picture of ships from that period, and which I think are in many ways similar to the Cypriote ship models, both larger merchant vessels and the smaller ones for more local needs.

When Odysseus had to leave Ogygia, Calypso gave him tools to build a boat. "Then she led the way to the borders of the island where tall trees were standing, alder and poplar and fir, reaching to the skies, long, dry and well-seasoned which would float for him lightly."[7] Odysseus then picked out twenty trees which he cut down and adzed to planks "and he bored all the pieces and fitted them to one another, and with pegs and morticings did he hammer it together"[8] making his ship "Wide as a man well-skilled in carpenting marks out the curve of the hull of a freight ship broad of beam. . ."[9]. He then set up the deck-beams by fastening them to close set frames and finished with long gunwales.[10] At last he equipped the boat with rudder, mast and sails.[11]

The ships of the Odyssey are often described as "hollow" which may also support the opinion of Casson that the ships were open with only a small deck fore and aft.[12] That the ship had at least a stern deck is certain. It is mentioned that during a gale the helmsman "like a diver he fell from the deck. . ."[13]

The mast was put in a mast-socket and held by two fore-stays. "The mast of fir they raised and set it in the hollow socket, and made it fast with fore-stays, and hauled up the white sail with twisted thongs of oxhide".[14] Mention of the rigging may also be found in the following lines: "and the blast of the wind snapped both the fore-stays of the mast"[15], and "but over the mast had been flung the back-stay fashioned of oxhide".[16]

The oar arrangement is indicated in the following verse: "and when you have all duly lashed the oars to the thole-pins"[17] and "fitted the oars in the leathern thole-straps, all in due order and spread the white sail".[18]

The size of one of the ships at last is indicated when fifty-two young men were chosen as crew.[19]

Morrison makes certain comparisons between the wrecks from Cape Gelidonya and Kyrenia and draws the conclusion that Odysseus' boat ought to have been 9 m. long.[20]

Earlier literature has considered Odysseus' boat as a raft but nowadays the general opinion is that Homer describes Odysseus making a boat, not a raft.[21]

With the often appearing epithets "swift" and "curved" one then gets a very clear and vivid picture of a fast-sailing ship, fitted with many oars and a big square white cloth sail held by twisted oxhide thongs.

Homer's account of how Odysseus built his boat as well as the details and aspects on the ships of the Odyssey correspond in many ways with the Cypriote ship models and perhaps especially with the ships in group 2.

CONCLUSION

The ships listed in this catalogue may be interpreted as representations of ships made and used mainly for peaceful purposes. Among them I have distinguished three groups, each reflecting the importance of transport by sea for various purposes. The first group of merchant ships are indirectly evidence of the central role of Cyprus as trade partner, with its own means of transporting such export products as copper, wine and other goods for long distances, and corresponding possibilities for importing from other countries.

The major category of the ships placed in the second group, which I consider to represent the typical Cypriote boat, is of smaller size than the ships in the first group. Even if the differences between the large and the small boats are small and vague it must be supposed that they were used for different purposes. The small boats were of course, used for less bulky cargoes and, also for shorter transports. Within this group can be found some models of boats with a low freeboard which can be regarded as coasters, built for transport of passengers and freight along the coast of Cyprus.

On the whole, the boats give a strong impression of the skill of the Cypriote boatbuilders and of the adaptation of the boats in size and qualities for trade across the seas, as well as for more local maritime activities such as household fishing and transport of animals.

Concerning construction and appearance, the Cypriote models of ships seem to follow the general tradition of boatbuilding in the eastern Mediterranean.

Tradition is strong in the art of shipbuilding and variations occurring are mostly local characteristics. For thousands of years the meltemi has blown from northwest during the summer season, and this constant element may perhaps have influenced the conservative development of shipbuilding. The conditions for today's sailor with an auxiliary motor and for the captain of a sailing vessel with oarsmen in antiquity are consequently not very different.

NOTES: CHAPTER VIII

1. J.S. Morrison, 'The Classical traditions' in B. Greenhill, *Archaeology of the boat*, London 1976, 158.
2. Casson, Pl. 78.
3. See S.C. Humphreys' review of Gray's book in *Classical Philology*, 71, January – October 1976, Chicago 1976, 347.
4. Casson, 44.
5. J.S. Morrison (supra note 1), 163.
6. Casson, 36.
7. Homer, *Odyssey*, 5.239–243.
8. Op. cit. 5.247–248.
9. Op. cit. 5.249–251.
10. Op. cit. 5.252–253.
11. Op. cit. 5.254–257.
12. Casson, 44.
13. Homer, *Odyssey*, 12.411–414.
14. Op. cit. 15.289–290.
15. Op. cit. 12.409–410.
16. Op. cit. 12.423.
17. Op. cit. 8.37.
18. Op. cit. 8.53.
19. Op. cit. 8.48–49.
20. J.S. Morrison (supra note 1), 163.
21. J.S. Morrison (supra note 1), 163; Casson, 217–219.

GLOSSARY OF NAUTICAL TERMS

based on A. Ansted's *A dictionary of sea terms.*

beam: the greatest width of a ship

belaying pin: fixed wooden pin to which lines are secured

bollard: upright post on a quay or a ship's deck for making ropes secure

bow: the front part of a ship

bulkhead: wall or partition

bulwark: parapet around an exposed deck

cathead: projecting timber from which the anchor can be slung

cutwater: the portion of a vessel's stem that cleaves the water as she moves

frames: appended to the keel, give the vessel its shape (as ribs do in the human torso)

freeboard: distance from the water level to the main deck

gunwale: the uppermost course of planking on a ship's side

halyard: rope for raising or lowering a sail

helmsman: the man who steers the vessel

hull: the body of a ship

keel: the backbone of a ship

kelson: an addition to the keel inside the boat

life-line: safety rope fastened along the top of the gunwale

l.o.a.: (=length over all) entire length from stem to stem

painter: rope for fastening a vessel alongside a quay etc.

poop or poop-deck: an extra deck on the after part of a ship

port: the left-hand side of a ship facing forward

prow: the front part of the bow

ram: a massive projection at the bow of a ship

scuppers: openings in the bulwarks of a ship to carry off the deck water

sheer: the straight or curved line which the deck of a vessel makes when viewed from the side

sheet or sheet-line: line attached to the lower parts of a sail

stanchions: upright posts for supporting life-lines

starboard: the right-hand side of a ship facing forward

stay: line to support a mast or spar

stem: properly the foremost timber of a vessel. Owing to the difficulty of deciding which end of some ships is the bow and which is the stern, I have consistently used the word "stem" also for what could have been the stern post

stern: the after part of a vessel
strake: a line of planking extending the length of a vessel
tholepin: pin against which the oar is worked
thwart: cross plank serving as seat for the oarsman
tumble-home: when a cross-section of the hull shows a narrower
  beam at deck level than further down
water-line: point on the hull reached by the water when the ship is
  floating normally
yard: spar along the head of a sail.

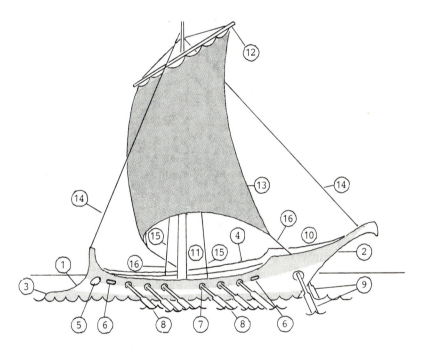

<table>
<tr><td>1. Bow</td><td>6. Scuppers</td><td>12. Yard</td></tr>
<tr><td>2. Stern</td><td>7. Oarholes</td><td>13. Sail</td></tr>
<tr><td>3. Ram</td><td>8. Oars</td><td>14. Stays</td></tr>
<tr><td>4. Gunwale</td><td>9. Steering oars</td><td>15. Halyards</td></tr>
<tr><td>5. Cathead</td><td>10. Poop-deck</td><td>16. Sheet lines</td></tr>
<tr><td></td><td>11. Mast</td><td></td></tr>
</table>

BIBLIOGRAPHY
see also ABBREVIATIONS page 3

Ansted, A., *A dictionary of sea terms*, Glasgow 1919.

Åström, P., *The Middle Cypriote Bronze Age*, Lund 1957.

Åström, P., 'Cypern – en kulturhistorisk och konsthistorisk skiss' in *Cypern – motsättningarnas ö*, Gothenburg 1974, (*SIMA* Pocket-book 1).

Barnett, R.D., 'Early shipping in the Near East in Antiquity', *Antiquity* 32, 1958.

Bass, G.F., *A history of seafaring based on underwater archaeology*, London 1972.

Blegen, C., 'Hyria', *Hesperia*, Supplement VIII, Athens 1949.

Boardman, J., *Greek gems and finger rings*, London 1970.

Bonino, M., 'Un modello di nave cipriota del sec. VI – V a. C.', *Rivista di Studi Liguri* 31, 1965.

Bossert, H. Th., *Altsyrien*, Tübingen 1951.

Caubet, A., Karageorghis, V. and Yon, M., *Les antiquités de Chypre, Age du Bronze*, Paris 1981, (Musée du Louvre, Département des antiquités orientales, Notes et Documents des musées de France 2).

Cesnola, L.P. di, *A descriptive Atlas of the Cesnola Collection of Cypriote Antiquities in the Metropolitan Museum of Art in New York* II, Boston 1885.

Frankel, D., 'A Middle Cypriote vessel with modelled figures from Politiko Lambertis', *RDAC* 1974.

Frost, H., 'From rope to chain: on the development of anchors in the Mediterranean', *The Mariner's Mirror* 49, 1963.

Gjerstad, E., *The Cypro-Geometric, Cypro-Archaic and Cypro-Classical periods*, *SCE* IV: 2, Stockholm 1948.

de Graeve, M. -Ch., *The ships of the ancient Near East (c.2000–500 B.C.)*, Leuven 1981.

Greenhill, B., *Archaeology of the boat*, London 1976.

Homer, *The Iliad*, with a translation by Murray, A. T. (The Loeb Classical Library), London – Cambridge 1946.

Homer, *The Odyssey*, with a translation by Murray, A.T. (The Loeb Classical Library), London – Cambridge 1946.

Humphreys, S.C., A review of Gray in *Classical Philology 71*, January–October 1976, Chicago 1976.

Johnson, J., *Maroni de Chypre*, Gothenburg 1980, (*SIMA* LIX).

Johnston, P.F., 'Bronze Age Cycladic ships', in *Temple University Aegean Symposium* 7, 1982.

Kapera, Z.J., 'Terakotowy model barki morskiej', *Rozprawy i Sprawozdania Muzeum Narodowego w Krakowie* 10, Cracow 1970.

Kapera, Z.J., 'Terakotowa flota Kinyrasa', *Bibliotheca Classica Orientalis* 14, Berlin 1969.

Karageorghis, V., *Salamis in Cyprus*, London 1969.

Karageorghis, V., *Excavations in the necropolis of Salamis* II, London 1970.

Karageorghis, V., and des Gagniers, J., *La céramique chypriote de style figuré*, Rome 1974, (Biblioteca di antichità cipriote 2) and Supplément, Rome 1979 (Biblioteca di antichità cipriote 5).

Karageorghis, V., *Kition*, London 1976.

Katzev, M.L., 'The Kyrenia ship' in G.F. Bass, *A history of seafaring based on underwater archaeology*, London 1972.

Landström, B., *Sailing ships*, London 1969.

McCaslin, D.E., 'The 1977 underwater report' in *HST* 4, Gothenburg 1978, (*SIMA* XLV:4).

McCaslin, D.E., *Stone anchors in Antiquity: Coastal settlements and maritime trade-routes in the Eastern Mediterranean ca. 1600–1050 B.C.*, Gothenburg 1980, (*SIMA* LXI).

Marinatos, S., 'Das Schiffsfresko von Akrotiri, Thera' in D. Gray, *Seewesen*, Göttingen 1974 (=*Archaeologia Homerica*, Band I, Kap. G.).

Merrillees, R.S., *Trade and transcendence in the Bronze Age Levant*, Gothenburg *1974, (SIMA* XXXIX).

Morrison, J.S., 'The Classical traditions' in B. Greenhill, *Archaeology of the boat*, London 1976.

Myres, J.L., *Handbook of the Cesnola Collection of Antiquities from Cyprus*, New York 1914.

Öbrink, U., *HST* 5, Gothenburg 1979, (*SIMA* XLV:5).

Ohnefalsch-Richter, M., *Kypros, die Bibel und Homer*, Berlin 1893.

Peltenburg, E.J., *Recent developments in the Later Prehistory of Cyprus*, Gothenburg 1982, (*SIMA* Pocket-book 16).

Schaeffer, C.F.A., *Missions en Chypre 1932–1935*, Paris 1936.

Schaeffer, C.F.A., *Enkomi-Alasia. Nouvelles missions en Chypre, 1946–1950*, Paris 1952.

Stieglitz, R.R., 'An ancient terra-cotta ship from Cyprus', *Sefunim* IV (1972–1975), Haifa.

Todd, I.A., 'Vasilikos Valley project: Second preliminary report 1977', *JFA* 5, 1978.

Todd, I.A., 'Vasilikos Valley project: Third preliminary report 1978', *JFA* 6, 1979.

Woolner, D., 'Graffiti of ships at Tarxien, Malta,' *Antiquity* 31, 1957.

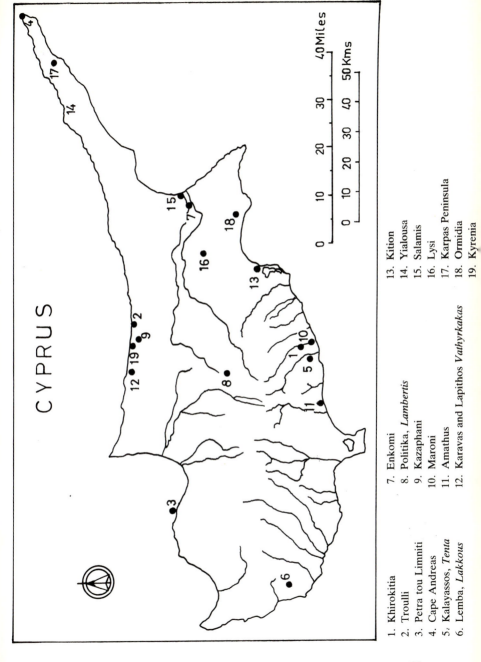

CYPRUS

40 Miles
50 Kms

0   10   20   30   40

0   10   20   30   40   50

1. Khirokitia
2. Troulli
3. Petra tou Limniti
4. Cape Andreas
5. Kalavassos, *Tenta*
6. Lemba, *Lakkous*

7. Enkomi
8. Politika, *Lambertis*
9. Kazaphani
10. Maroni
11. Amathus
12. Karavas and Lapithos *Vathyrkakas*

13. Kition
14. Yialousa
15. Salamis
16. Lysi
17. Karpas Peninsula
18. Ormidia
19. Kyrenia

Fig. 1

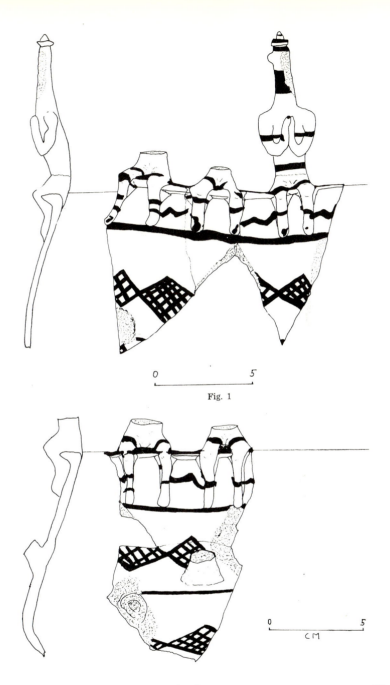

Fig. 1

0   5

0   5
CM

Fig. 2

77

Fig. 3

Fig. 4

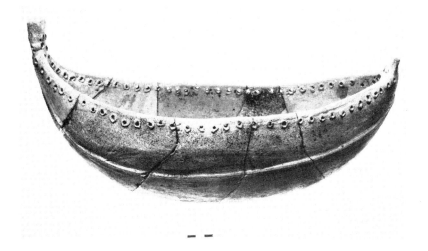

Fig. 5

Fig. 7

Fig. 6

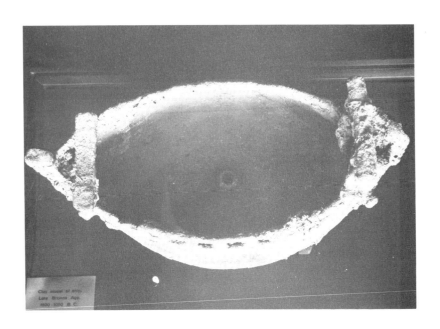

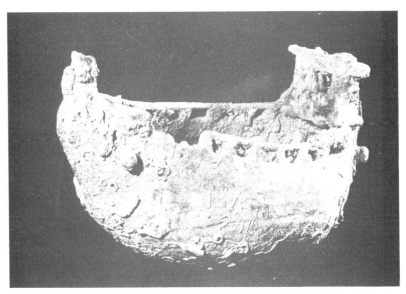

Fig. 8

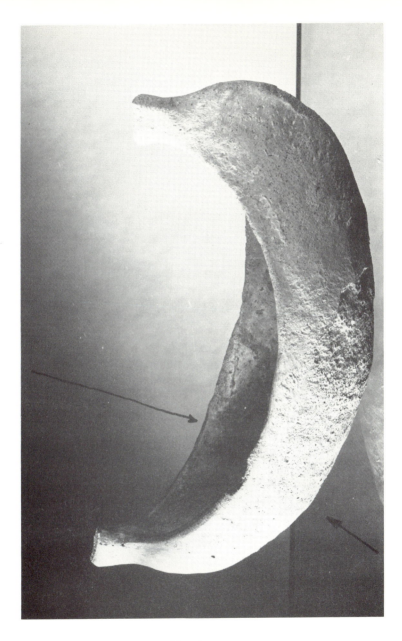

Fig. 9

Fig. 10

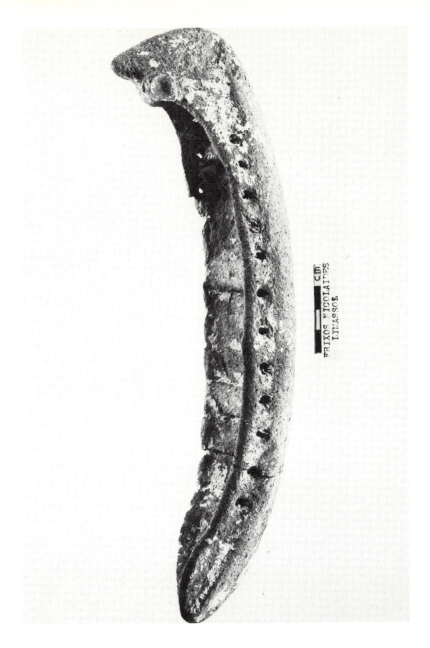

Fig. 11

Fig. 12

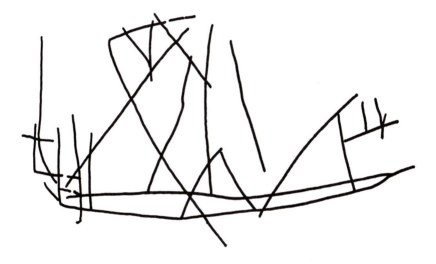

Fig. 13

Fig. 14

Fig. 15

Fig. 16

Fig. 17

Fig. 18

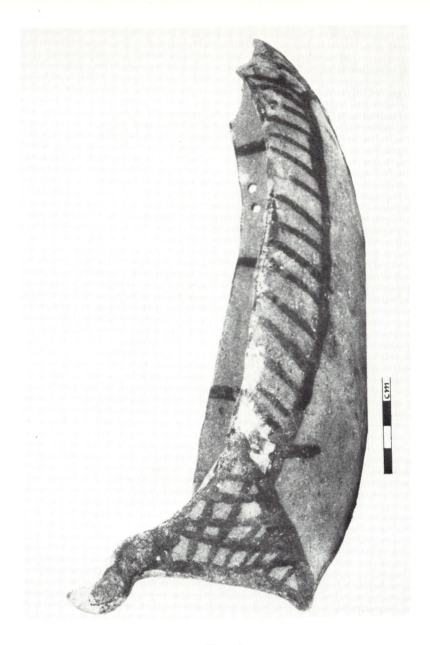

Fig. 19

Fig. 20

92

Fig. 21

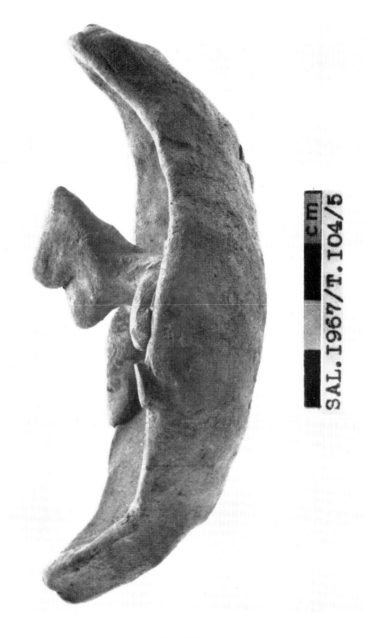

Fig. 22

Fig. 23

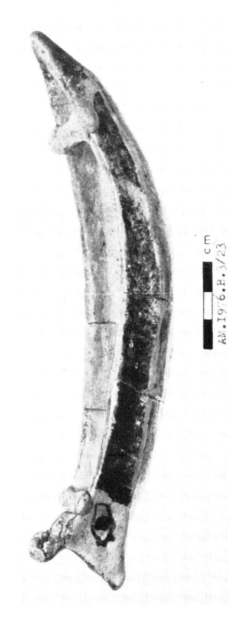

Fig. 24

Fig. 25

Fig. 26

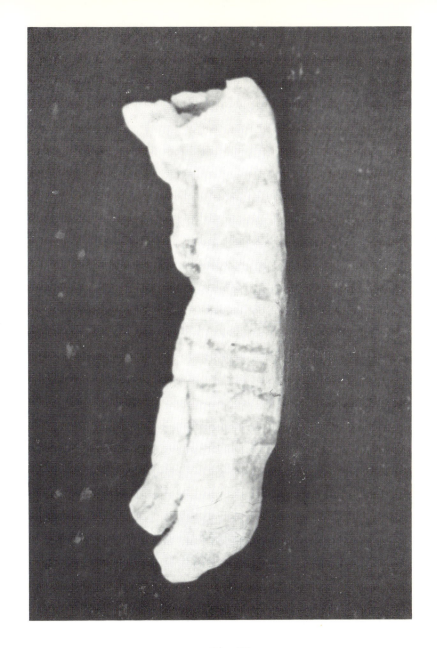

Fig. 27

Fig. 28

Fig. 29

Fig. 30

Fig. 31   Fig. 33

Fig. 32

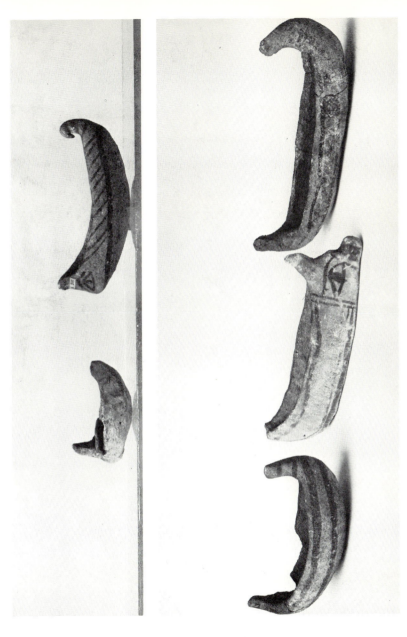

Fig. 37, 39   Fig. 36, 40, 34

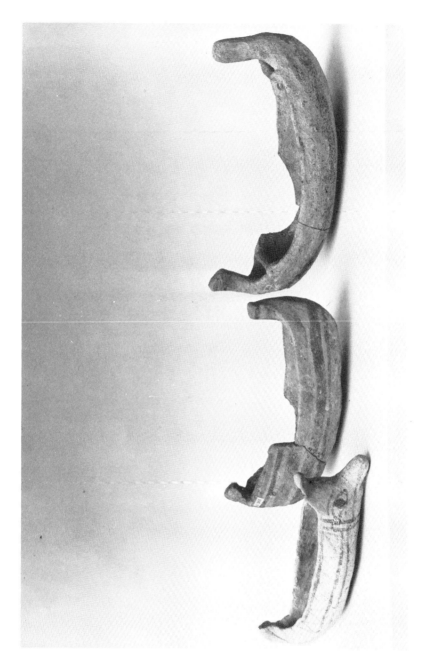

Fig. 41, 35, 31

Fig. 38

Fig. 43, 42

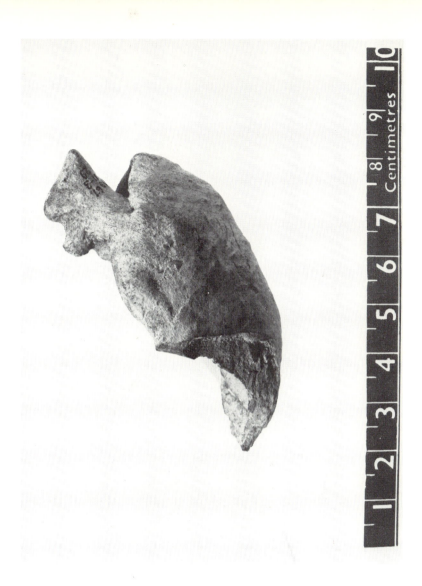

Fig. 44

107

Fig. 45

Fig. 46

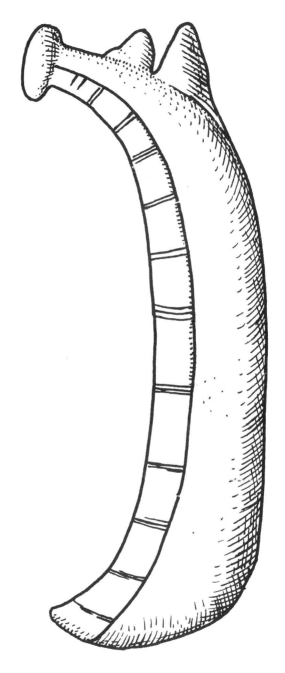

Fig. 47

Fig. 48

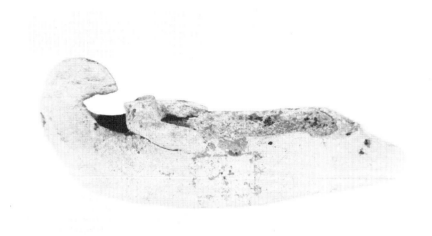

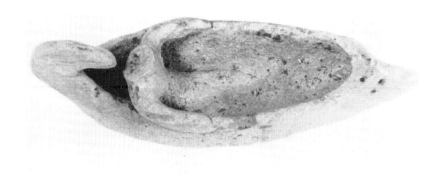

Fig. 49

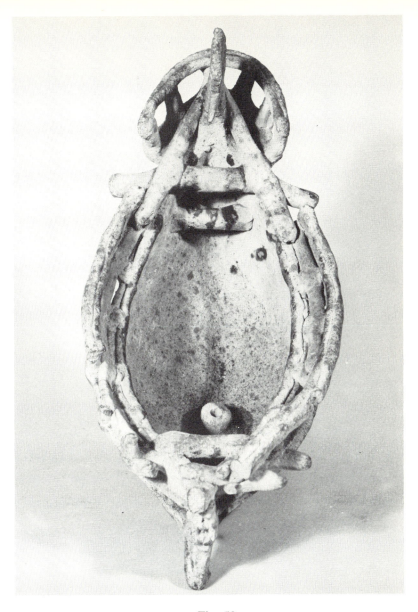

Fig. 50

The Metropolitan Museum of Art, The Cesnola Collection; Purchased by subscription, 1874–76.

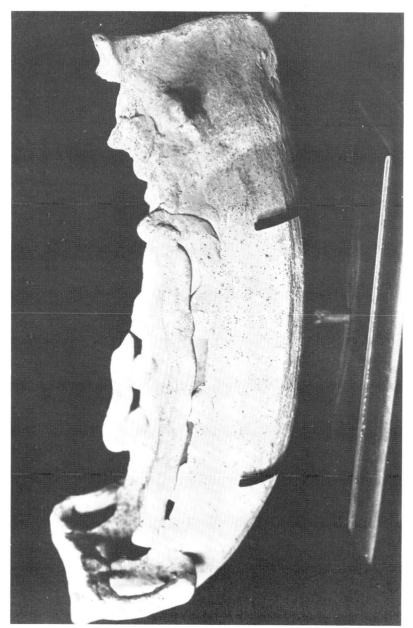

Fig. 51

The Metropolitan Museum of Art, Cesnola Collection; Purchased by subscription,   1874–76.

Fig. 52

The Metropolitan Museum of Art, The Cesnola Collection; Purchased
by subscription,   1874–76.

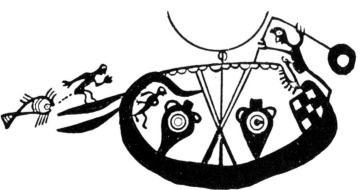

Fig. 53

Fig. 54

Fig. 55

The Metropolitan Museum of Art, Cesnola Collection; Purchased by subscription, 1874–76. (74.51.511.)

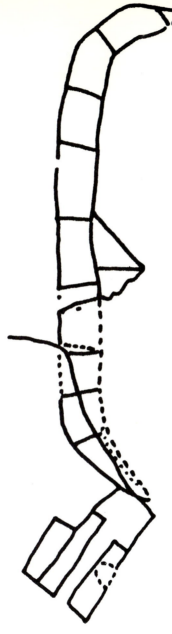

Fig. 56